דעת תבונות

The Wisdom of Consciousness

A Dialogue Between the
Soul and the Intellect

By

The Ramchal
Rabbi Moshe Chaim Luzzatto

Translated by
Rav Raphael Afilalo

Hazohar555@gmail.com

kabbalah5.com - zoharvideos.com – ramchal.com

YouTube: Rav Raphael Afilalo – Zohar - Kabbalah

ISBN: 978-2-9822170-0-3

Previous publications by Rav Raphael Afilalo

English

Concepts of Kabbalah
Kabbalah Dictionary
Glossary of Kabbalah
Arizal Prince of the
Kabbalists
160 Questions on the
Kabbalah
Kabbalah of the Arizal,
according to the Ramhal
Gates of Reincarnations

French

Concepts de Kabbalah
Dictionnaire de Kabbalah
Glossaire de Kabbalah
Arizal Prince des
Kabbalistes
160 Questions sur la
Kabbalah
Kabbalah du Arizal, selon
le Ramhal
Portes des Réincarnations

Translations of books of the Ramchal

God and His Ways
The Kabbalist and the
Philosopher
The Way of the Sinceres
The Wisdom of
Consciousness

Dieu et Ses Voies
Le Kabbaliste et le
Philosophe
La Voie des Sincères
La Sagesse Ultime de la
Conscience

בעברית

מושגי חכמת הקבלה

חשיבות לימוד הזהר

אריז״ל נשיא המקובלים

קיצור כתבי הארי

קבלה – תורה האמת

הזהר – כתבים מיסטיים של פנמיוה התורה

THE LIFE OF THE RAMCHAL 7

INTRODUCTION 11

TO UNDERSTAND THE FUNDAMENTAL PRINCIPLES OF FAITH......... 15

THE PURPOSE OF MAN'S EXISTENCE AND SERVICE........................ 17

THE CREATION OF EVIL AND ITS BOUNDARIES 44

THE GENERAL PROVIDENCE TOWARD MAN 47

THE CONCEALMENT AND ILLUMINATION OF GOD'S FACE 52

THE DOMINION OF THE SOUL AND BODY IN DIFFERENT STATES 67

THE THREE STATES OF THE WORLD 73

MAN'S SERVICE IN THIS WORLD 75

THE EXISTENCE OF EVIL AND ITS ROLE 79

THE ORDERS OF PROVIDENCE IN REWARD AND PUNISHMENT 93

ORDER OF THE RECTIFICATION OF THE WORLD 109

REWARD AND PUNISHMENT 115

THE CHANGING ESSENCE OF THE LOWER REALMS 132

PARTNERSHIP BETWEEN THE RIGHTEOUS AND GOD....................137

THE SERVICE OF THE RIGHTEOUS AND ISRAEL............................145

REWARD AND PUNISHMENT WILL BE FOR THE WORLD TO COME.160

PROPHECY - ITS NATURE AND WAY 167

THE BOOKS OF THE RAMCHAL 187

DESCRIPTION OF SOME BOOKS OF THE RAMCHAL 188

SAMPLES OF BOOKS OF THE RAMCHAL TRANSLATED BY RAV RAPHAEL AFILALO 194

THE WAY OF THE JUSTS – MESILAT YESHARIM 194

GOD AND HIS WAYS - DEREKH HASHEM...................................... 210

THE KABBALIST AND THE PHILOSOPHER - MEAMAR HAVIKUACH . 222

The life of the Ramchal

Moshe Chaim Luzzatto, known as the Ramchal, was an enigmatic figure in Jewish history, remembered as a philosopher, kabbalist, and poet whose works have had a lasting impact on Jewish thought and mysticism. Born in Padua, Italy, on April 26, 1707, into a distinguished family, Ramchal displayed prodigious intellectual capabilities from a young age.

His education was comprehensive, steeped in the dual worlds of Jewish and secular knowledge, which was a hallmark of the Italian Jewish renaissance. He was well-versed in the Torah, Talmud, and Kabbalistic literature, as well as the sciences and philosophy of his time, which informed his unique approach to Jewish theology and ethics.

The Ramchal's intellectual journey began with his study of the Talmud and other classic Jewish texts, but he was particularly drawn to the study of Kabbalah, the Jewish mystical tradition. By the age of 20, he had already begun writing his own commentaries on these subjects. His most famous work, "Mesillat Yesharim" (Path of the Just), is a systematic exploration of Jewish ethics and spiritual growth, which has become a foundational text in the Mussar movement, a Jewish ethical, educational, and cultural movement.

Despite his young age, the Ramchal's works, such as "Derech Hashem" (God and His Ways), which systematically presents the fundamentals of Jewish belief, demonstrated a mastery of Jewish law and mysticism that few could rival. He also penned "Da'at Tevunot" (The Knowing Heart), a dialogue between the intellect and the soul on the nature of God's interaction with the world, and the purpose of Creation and human existence.

However, the Ramchal's intense involvement with Kabbalah, at a time when skepticism towards mysticism was widespread following the false messianic movement of Shabbetai Zvi, aroused suspicion. His formation of a select group of disciples to study Kabbalah led to further controversy. In 1727, under communal pressure in Italy, he agreed to a ban on teaching Kabbalah and ceased writing Kabbalistic works. This period of conflict was difficult for the Ramchal, whose only desire was to elevate the spiritual state of his people.

In search of a more accommodating environment for his Kabbalistic pursuits, Ramchal left Italy in 1735, eventually settling in Amsterdam. There, he hoped to live a life of spiritual and intellectual freedom. He supported himself by working as a diamond cutter and continued to write extensively. Amsterdam's Jewish community was a center of publishing, and it was there that he printed many of his works.

The Ramchal's life in Amsterdam allowed him some respite from the controversies that had followed him in Italy, and he continued his prolific writing, including works on Hebrew grammar and logic, such as "Sefer haHigayon" (The Book of Logic), which reflected his broader academic interests.

Despite his relatively comfortable life in Amsterdam, the Ramchal's longing for the Land of Israel was intense. In 1743, he and his family made the arduous journey to the Holy Land, settling in Acre. Tragically, his time there was short-lived; he died in a plague along with his family in 1746, at the young age of 39.

The Ramchal left behind a literary legacy that spans philosophical treatises, ethical texts, kabbalistic writings, poetry, plays, and more. His works continue to be studied for their depth and insight into the human condition and the divine.

Perhaps the most enduring aspect of the Ramchal's work is his ability to synthesize the mystical and rational aspects of Judaism. He believed that an understanding of the divine structure of the universe could lead to a profound religious life rooted in ethical conduct. His works have been embraced by various streams of Jewish thought, from the rationalist to the mystic, each finding in his writings a wellspring of knowledge and inspiration.

The legacy of the Ramchal is marked by a balance between the esoteric and the practical, the heavenly and the earthly. His vision of spiritual ascent is not one of withdrawal from the world but of engagement with it, guided by divine wisdom. His life and works serve as a bridge, inviting each person to traverse the gap between the finite and infinite, between human and divine potential.

The *Maggid* of Mezritch said:
 "His generation did not merit this great man…. Many among our people, through lack of knowledge, have uttered on this saintly man calumny that was not justified."

The Gaon of Vilna declared that if Ramchal was still alive, he would have traveled to Italy on foot to learn from his wisdom.

Moshe Chaim Luzzatto's contributions to Jewish thought and his teachings are now universally recognized as treasures of Jewish literature, offering guidance to those who seek a path of righteousness, intellect, and spiritual introspection. The Ramchal remains a beacon of spiritual and moral guidance, whose influence continues to be felt centuries after his passing.

Introduction

The profound dialogue between the Soul and the Intellect, as presented in this remarkable text, delves into the very essence of Jewish faith and philosophy. This work, a masterpiece of Jewish thought, explores the fundamental principles of Judaism, grappling with the most challenging questions that have perplexed the minds of believers throughout history. The author, Rabbi Moshe Chaim Luzzatto, through the use of a captivating dialogue format, guides the reader on a transformative journey, addressing the complexities of God's existence, the purpose of creation, the nature of good and evil, and the ultimate destiny of humankind.

At its core, this text is a testament to the unwavering faith of the Jewish people and their relentless pursuit of truth and understanding. The Soul, representing the innate yearning for spiritual connection and enlightenment, seeks guidance from the Intellect, the embodiment of wisdom and rational inquiry. Together, they embark on a quest to unravel the mysteries of the universe and the human condition, drawing upon the rich tapestry of Jewish scriptures, rabbinic literature, and philosophical thought. The dialogue begins with an exploration of the Thirteen Principles of Faith, as articulated by the renowned Jewish philosopher Maimonides. These principles serve as the bedrock of Jewish belief, encompassing the essential tenets of God's existence, unity, incorporeality, and eternity. The Soul and the Intellect meticulously examine each principle, providing compelling arguments and insights that strengthen the reader's understanding and conviction in these fundamental truths.

As the dialogue progresses, the text delves into the perplexing issue of theodicy – the presence of evil and suffering in a world created by a benevolent and omnipotent God. The Soul grapples with the age-old question of why the righteous suffer while the wicked prosper, seeking to reconcile this apparent injustice with the concept of divine providence. The Intellect, through a series of profound explanations and analogies, reveals the hidden wisdom behind God's ways, emphasizing the ultimate justice that will be served and the role of evil as a preparation for a greater good.

The purpose of creation and the role of humankind within the grand cosmic scheme is another central theme explored in this text. The Soul yearns to understand the reason for its existence and the ultimate goal of its earthly journey. The Intellect, drawing upon the rich tradition of Jewish thought, presents a compelling vision of God's desire to benefit His creatures and the unique opportunity granted to human beings to perfect themselves through their own efforts. The text emphasizes the importance of repairing deficiencies, both within oneself and in the world at large, as a means of attaining closeness to God and fulfilling one's divine purpose.

The nature of the soul and its relationship to the physical body is another fascinating topic addressed in this dialogue. The Soul seeks to comprehend its own essence and the reason for its descent into the material realm. The Intellect, through a series of profound insights, reveals the soul's lofty source and its mission to refine and elevate the body. The text explores the concept of resurrection and the various levels of existence, providing a glimpse into the ultimate destiny of the human soul and its reunion with its divine origin.

The interplay between good and evil, and the nature of divine influence in the world, is another central theme of this text. The Soul grapples with the question of how a perfect God could allow for the existence of evil and imperfection. The Intellect, through a series of intricate arguments, reveals the root of good and evil and the delicate balance of divine influences that shape the course of creation. The text emphasizes the role of human free will and the importance of aligning oneself with the forces of goodness and holiness.

As the dialogue reaches its climax, the text explores the concepts of divine guidance, rectification, and the ultimate revelation of God's unity. The Soul learns of the critical role played by the righteous individuals, the Tzaddikim, in repairing the world and bringing about the final redemption. The Intellect reveals the intricate workings of divine providence, the synthesis of reward and punishment, and the importance of maintaining faith amidst apparent injustice.

The final sections of the text delve into the profound topics of prophecy and the process of creation itself. The Soul seeks to understand the nature and purpose of prophetic visions, and the Intellect provides a lucid explanation of how God communicates His will to humankind through the medium of prophecy. The text also explores the concept of God's innovation of existence, the divine influences that shape the cosmos, and the ultimate actualization of creation.

Throughout this captivating dialogue, the reader is challenged to grapple with the most profound questions of human existence and to seek a deeper understanding of God's ways. The text is a testament to the enduring power of Jewish faith and the indomitable spirit of human inquiry. It is a call to action, urging each individual to take up the mantle of spiritual growth and to play an active role in the perfection of the world.

In conclusion, this masterpiece of Jewish thought is a treasure trove of wisdom and insight, offering a roadmap for the soul's journey towards truth and enlightenment. It is a work that demands careful study and contemplation, inviting the reader to embark on a transformative journey of self-discovery and spiritual growth. As the Soul and the Intellect conclude their dialogue, the reader is left with a renewed sense of purpose and a deeper appreciation for the beauty and complexity of the Jewish faith. This text is a timeless classic that will continue to inspire and guide generations of seekers, as they strive to unravel the mysteries of the universe and to draw closer to the divine presence that animates all of creation.

Rav Raphael Afilalo

To Understand the Fundamental Principles of Faith

Soul: My desire and will is to settle on some of the things about which it is said (Deuteronomy 4:39), "And you shall know this day and consider it in your heart, that the Lord, He is God," for these are among the fundamentals of our faith which every person is obligated to pursue, to the best of their ability.

Intellect: Where are you heading? The principles are thirteen - on which of them do you wish to contemplate?

Soul: All thirteen principles are validated to me without any doubt; but some are both verified and understood, while others are verified by faith but not clarified through understanding and knowledge.

Intellect: Which are verified to you, and which are clarified to you?

Soul: The existence, unity, eternity, incorporeality and immateriality of God, the creation of the world, prophecy, the prophecy of Moshe, and the Torah from heaven and its eternity - I believe and understand all these without need for further clarification. But providence, reward and punishment, the coming of the Messiah and resurrection of the dead - I believe due to religious obligation, but would like to have a reason to be at ease with them.

Intellect: What difficulties do you have with these matters?

Soul: The great causes overturning in the world that seem to show the opposite of providence, God forbid. Especially since reason cannot see the end and purpose of things, how God leads His creatures, and what is the ultimate aim; for the deeds of the blessed God have such latitude that no heart can contain them. I would like you to teach me a straight path to understand the uprightness of these matters, without turning right or left.

Intellect: There are very difficult and profound issues here, such as the righteous suffering and the wicked prospering, which have troubled even the greatest sages and prophets, including Moshe. They cannot be fully comprehended.

Soul: I will leave the incomprehensible details. But at least provide me with upright general principles, so I may have counsel and reason amidst the latitude of these matters. What my knowledge does not reach, I will accept is not for me to complete.

Intellect: It is certain that the Holy One, blessed be He, established His world on justice and upright, faithful conduct, as the faithful shepherd testified (Deuteronomy 32:4), "The Rock, His work is perfect, for all His ways are justice; a God of faithfulness and without iniquity, just and right is He."

Soul: The uprightness of this justice and depth of this perfect counsel is what I desire to hear explained clearly.

The Purpose of Man's Existence and Service

Intellect: First we must clarify the matter of human existence and the service incumbent upon man, to understand the desired purpose in all this.

Soul: This certainly requires much contemplation to understand clearly in all its parts.

Intellect: The first foundation on which the entire structure stands is that the supreme will wanted man to perfect himself and all creatures for his sake - this itself will be his merit and reward. His merit is that he engages in and labors to attain this perfection, enjoying the fruits of his own efforts. His reward is that he himself will be perfected and delight in goodness forever.

Soul: This foundation includes many angles. I await to hear what you will build upon it, so I may comprehensively discern what it includes. But first, is there a reason why the supreme will wanted this?

Intellect: The reason is simple, and depends on the answer to another question - why did the blessed Creator want to create creatures?

Soul: You answer a matter that is equal for both of us.

Intellect: What we can comprehend is that God, the ultimate good, wanted to create creatures in order to benefit them, for if there are no recipients of good, there is no beneficence. For the beneficence to be complete, He knew in His lofty wisdom that the recipients should receive it through their own efforts, becoming owners of that good without shame, unlike one who receives charity. On this they said (Jerusalem Talmud, Orlah 1:3), "He who eats that which is not his own is ashamed to look at his face."

Soul: The reason settles in my heart. Now complete your words.

Intellect: From this premise emerges a great root to contemplate - the matter of deficiency and its perfection. We need to know what the deficiency is, its consequences, the rectification by which creation is perfected, the way of doing this rectification, and its consequences.

Soul: But I think we first need to understand the perfection man will attain when he has completed his work and rested from his labor. Then we can understand in retrospect all that we have mentioned, for what man ultimately attains is what he initially lacked and needs to strive to acquire.

Intellect: You have spoken correctly. We can now understand perfection in general, not in detail, but this general knowledge will allow us to understand the deficiencies in detail, for every deficiency is the absence of that perfection.

Soul: Say what you have to say about this perfection.

Intellect: This perfection is simple from Scripture and reason; it is that man will cleave to God's holiness and enjoy the perception of His glory without any hindrance or obstruction. As it is written (Isaiah 58:14), "Then you shall delight in the Lord"; (Psalms 140:14), "The upright shall dwell in Your presence"; (Ibid. 16:11), "Fullness of joys in Your presence," and many others like these throughout the words of the prophets and writings, revealed to all nations. In the words of our Sages (Berachot 17a), "The World to Come has no eating or drinking etc., but the righteous sit with their crowns on their heads and delight in the radiance of the Divine Presence."

Reason also dictates this, for the soul is a portion of God above, and its desire is certainly to return and cleave to its source, as is the nature of every effect that yearns for its cause and has no rest until it attains this. But the nature of this cleaving and attainment we do not have the power to understand amidst our current deficiencies. From this we discern that our deficiencies are the distance and hindrance interposing between us and God, making it impossible to cleave to Him as we will after the hindrance passes. This is the deficiency we need to strive to remove from ourselves in order to acquire the perfection we mentioned.

Soul: The reason settles in my heart. Now complete your words.

Intellect: Before proceeding, we must clarify the existence of man and the service incumbent upon him, to understand the desired purpose in all this.

Soul: This matter certainly requires much contemplation to understand it clearly in all its parts.

Intellect: The foundation on which everything stands is that the supreme will wanted man to perfect himself and all that was created for his sake; this will be his merit and reward. His merit - because he is found to be engaged and laboring to attain this perfection; when he attains it - he will enjoy the fruit of his labor and his share of all his toil. His reward - for he will be the perfected one, delighting in goodness forever.

Soul: This foundation includes many facets. I am waiting to hear what you will build upon it, so I may discern in retrospect what is included. But first, is there a reason why the supreme will wanted this?

Intellect: The reason is simple; it depends on the answer to another question: why did the blessed Creator want to create creatures?

Soul: You answer a matter that is equal for both of us.

Intellect: What we can comprehend is that God, may He be blessed, is the ultimate good. It is the law of good to do good; this is what He wanted - to create creatures so that He could benefit them. For if there is no recipient of good, there is no beneficence. For the beneficence to be complete, He knew in His lofty wisdom that it is fitting for the recipients to receive it through their own effort, making them the owners of that good, not remaining with shame in receiving it, like one who receives charity. On this they said (Jerusalem Talmud, Orlah, Chapter 1, Halacha 3), "He who eats that which is not his own is ashamed to look at his face."

Soul: The reason settles in my heart. Now complete your words.

Intellect: From this premise, a great root emerges for us to contemplate: the matter of deficiency and its perfection. We need to know what deficiency is, its consequences, its rectification by which creation will be perfected, the way of doing this rectification, and its consequences.

Soul: I think we first need to understand the perfection that man will attain when he has completed his work and rested from his labor. Then we will understand in retrospect all that we have mentioned. The reason is simple and clear: what man will ultimately attain is what he lacked initially, and because he lacks it, he needs to strive and acquire it.

Intellect: You have spoken correctly. We can now understand perfection in general, not in detail, but by knowing it in general, we will understand the deficiencies in detail in retrospect, for every deficiency is the absence of that perfection.

Soul: Say what you have to say about this perfection.

Intellect: This perfection is simple from Scripture and reason; it is that man will cleave to His holiness, and enjoy the perception of His glory without any hindrance or separating force. As it is written, "Then you shall delight in the Lord"; "The upright shall abide in Your presence"; "In Your presence is fullness of joy," and many others like these, revealed in the words of the prophets and the writings. In the words of our Sages, of blessed memory, "In the World to Come, the righteous sit with their crowns on their heads and delight in the radiance of the Divine Presence."

A logical reason: the soul is a portion of God above, and its desire is to return and cleave to its source to comprehend it, as is the nature of every effect that yearns for its cause, having no rest until it attains this. But what this cleaving and comprehension will be - we do not have the power to understand as long as we are in the midst of deficiencies. From this, we discern our deficiencies, for just as perfection is this cleaving, the deficiencies are all the distance and hindrance that interposes between us and Him, making it impossible to cleave to Him as we will after the hindrance passes. This is the deficiency we need to strive to remove to acquire the perfection we mentioned.

Here we need a very fundamental premise.

Soul: What is it?

Intellect: That God, blessed be He, was certainly able to create man and all creation with ultimate perfection; it would have been fitting for it to be so, for Him being perfect in all kinds of perfection - it is fitting that His deeds should be perfect in all perfection. But when His wisdom decreed to leave man to perfect himself, He created these creatures lacking perfection. This is as if He restrained His attribute of perfection and His great goodness from acting according to the law of His greatness in these creatures, but to make them in the disposition He wanted according to the purpose intended in His lofty thought. Here is included another knowledge, as they said, "Shaddai - that He said to His world 'enough'"; that the heavens were stretching and going until He rebuked them, as written in the Midrash. Certainly, He could have created more and greater creatures than He did; if He had wanted to create His creatures according to the proportion of the Creator, they would have had no measure, just as He and His ability have no measure. But He created them according to the proportion of the created, measuring in them the fitting disposition for them according to what was intended. In any case, He certainly restrained, as it were, His great and infinite ability, so that it would not act in His creatures like its proportion, but according to the proportion of these creatures that are acted upon by it.

Soul: All this is certainly necessary, for it is of the faith that God, may His name be blessed, is omnipotent in all ways; it is impossible to set any limit or measure to His ability. Everything we see that was created from Him in a specific and limited measure - it will not be according to His proportion, God forbid, but according to what His will decreed to act.

Intellect: Let us establish this principle, then proceed to another fundamental premise. This principle: the Master has certainly prevented Himself, as it were, meaning that He prevented His ability in creating His creatures, not making them according to His power, but according to what He wanted and intended for them; He created them lacking so that they themselves would complete themselves, their perfection being their reward in the merit of their efforts to attain it. All this only because He wanted to bestow a complete beneficence.

Soul: Now let us hear this premise that you mentioned.

Intellect: The first premise we need to understand is where man's power is found to perfect his deficiencies, since he was created deficient. We are now entering a very great and wide sea, for we will need many great propositions before coming to complete our subject. You need to be very patient, to understand the matters in proper order, for this is the way of wisdom - to acquire knowledge one after another, until in the end everything will come to light as one complete matter, for which all those premises were needed.

Soul: Speak your words in the proper order, I am listening with all the patience and resolve required.

Intellect: First, you need to know that even though we have said that the blessed Master wanted to give perception of the essence of His perfection to His creatures, it is certainly not the will to give them perception of all His perfection which has no end, limit, or boundary; but on the contrary, only a small edge of it He wanted to reveal to them, in which will be all their delight in attaining it, as we have explained. This is very simple and desirable, for it is impossible for a consequent and created being like us to comprehend all the perfection of the Creator as it is said, "Can you by searching find out God? Can you find out the Almighty unto perfection?" It is found that all that creatures can attain will certainly not be even like a drop from the great sea of the perfection of the Creator, may He be blessed.

Soul: This is simple to all wise of heart, as it has been said, (Psalms 106:2), "Who can express the mighty acts of the Lord," etc.

Intellect: Now, when we consider all the orders of His deeds, all the great deeds He has done since placing man upon the earth, all that He has promised us to do through His holy prophets, what becomes clear to us with absolute clarity is the intensity of His unity. We see that all the other attributes of His perfection which have no end are not clarified to us at all, for we do not have the power to comprehend them. For example, we know that He is wise, but we have not comprehended the end of His wisdom; we know that He knows, but we have not comprehended His knowledge. Therefore they said, (Prayer of Elijah, Tikunei Zohar, Second Introduction), "You are wise, but not with a known wisdom, You are understanding, but not with a known understanding." Since we cannot comprehend these attributes, it follows that we are prohibited from investigating them, for about all such things it is said (Chagigah 13a in the name of Ben Sira 3:21), "You shall not seek what is too wonderful for you, you shall not investigate what is concealed from you"; so they said, (Sefer Yetzirah, Chapter 1), "If your heart runs - return to the place."

But His unity, on the contrary, is revealed and clarified to us with complete clarity. It follows that not only is it clarified to us, but we are obligated to consider this knowledge, to implant it in our hearts with complete resolve without any doubt at all. This is what Moshe our teacher, peace be upon him, commanded us from the mouth of the Almighty (Deuteronomy 4:39), "Know therefore this day, and consider it in your heart, that the Lord He is God in heaven above, and upon the earth beneath; there is none else."

The supreme mouth testifies of Himself and informs that all that is gathered from all His great causes with which He overturns in His world, is the revelation of this complete unity; as it is said, (Deuteronomy 32:39), "See now that I, even I, am He, and there is no god with Me," this verse was said after He included the entire cycle of the wheel, which was destined and prepared to revolve in the world, all included in the words of the song of Ha'azinu, as the plain meaning of the verses proves.
He sealed the conclusion of His vision with this language, "See now that I, even I, am He," etc. In the words of the prophet Isaiah, it is clarified explicitly (Isaiah 43:10-11), "That you may know and believe Me, understand that I am He; before Me

there was no God formed, neither shall any be after Me. I, even I, am the Lord, and beside Me there is no savior"; as it is written (Isaiah 44:6), "I am the first, I am the last, and beside Me there is no God"; as it is written (Isaiah 44:6-7, "That they may know from the rising of the sun, and from the west, that there is none beside Me; I am the Lord, and there is none else; I form the light, and create darkness; I make peace, and create evil; I am the Lord, that does all these things." "That they may know," "that you may know and understand" it is written, implying that He wants us to know with knowledge and understanding. The ultimate of all the success that He promises to Israel is the clarification of His unity to the eyes of all. This matter is mentioned countless times in the words of the prophets, peace be upon them (Isaiah 2:11), "And the Lord alone shall be exalted in that day"; Zechariah 14:9), "And the Lord shall be king... in that day shall the Lord be One, and His name one"; (Zephaniah 3:9), "For then will I turn to the peoples a pure language, that they may all call upon the name of the Lord, to serve Him with one consent." In the end, this is our testimony every day continually (Deuteronomy 6:4), "Hear, O Israel: The Lord our God, the Lord is one."

It is found that all that is truly clarified to us from the intensity of His infinite perfection is only His complete unity. When we look with a contemplative gaze at all the deeds that have been done under the heavens, we see one course that revolves and goes, its rest being only the revelation of this truth. Now we need to understand this unity, what is desired in it, as the verse commanded us, (Deuteronomy 4:39), "and consider it in your heart that the Lord He is God," etc., implying that it requires the resolve of the mind and proper counsel in this matter. I have already said, this is a great and wide sea, in which we have to sail to our heart's content.

Soul: Until now you have prefaced a premise necessary for everything we will engage in in this debate of ours. Now let us come to our subject.

Intellect: The first time we now have to explain is the time of the concealment of His unity, as it is this day, the general time of man's service, as we have explained. From the law of His perfection, as we have said, He was certainly able to make all His works perfect, with nothing in His works but complete and perfect goodness, without any deficiency and evil at all. However, when He wanted to conduct Himself with His creatures with this conduct that we have mentioned, He innovated a completely new order, not according to the law of the supreme perfection, blessed be He, but what is necessary for the creatures to give them merit and good reward in their end.

It is the way of good and evil, reward and punishment; according to this way, good and evil are equal and come together in this world, good is prepared for the good just as evil is for the wicked; according to this way, creatures are sometimes corrupted, sometimes rectified, permission is given to Satan to incite, to the destroyer to destroy those whom God condemns, the nations of the world and idol worshippers are found, as well as all the other evils in the world, about which the promises of the prophets, peace be upon them, came to remove them from the world in the future, as it is said (Isaiah 2:18), "And the idols shall utterly pass away"; (Zechariah 13:2), "And the unclean spirit will I cause to pass out of the land"; (Isaiah 25:8), "He will swallow up death for ever";(Isaiah 11:9; 65:25), "They shall not hurt nor destroy in all My holy mountain," etc. According to the way, (Berachot 33b), "Everything is in the hands of Heaven except the fear of Heaven" - the Holy One, blessed be He, does not want to withhold anything in the hands of men if they want to corrupt their deeds. From this were born all the great corruptions in the world since the day that God created man; there is no rest for the righteous in this world, for man's evil is great upon him, Satan denounces at all times, the Holy One, blessed be He, is exacting with His pious ones like a hairbreadth. This is the general way that the supreme will innovated according to the matter of the concealment of His dominion and unity, depending only on the concealment of the countenance of His goodness, for if He had wanted to reveal Himself in the truth of His dominion, He would have removed all these evils, leaving only the good and the rectification alone, as He will do in the future to come.

Know further, that certainly even now, even though He concealed His goodness and withheld the law of His perfection from the creatures, He still bestows upon them, for from where would they have existence, being, and sustenance if not from His bestowal. He certainly bestows, but this bestowal that He bestows now - compared to what would have been fitting for

Him to bestow if He had wanted to bestow according to the law of His perfection - is nothing but like the likeness of a shadow compared to a man, or like a small impression that remains from the writing on the paper after the letters have departed from it. The general kind of this bestowal is called darkness and not light, compared to the perfect bestowal that could have come if He had bestowed according to the law of His perfection. However, compared to us, this is all our life, for in this bestowal we live and exist, not otherwise. It is found that when we mention the kind of this innovated bestowal in the concealment of His countenance of goodness, we will call it in one general term - only like the shadow of the supreme power, no more; in its details - we will find in it all the laws and judgments that we discern in the supreme conduct, for all of them together are considered a very small thing compared to the supreme power if it were acting in its perfection, as I have mentioned.

Soul: Summarize what you have explained so far.

Intellect: The Holy One, blessed be He, restrained His attribute of perfection in creating these creatures, making them lacking rather than perfect. He set for them a way of conduct and bestowal that is but the darkness of His concealment, giving rise to the balance of good and evil, sins, blemishes, punishments and corruptions. Yet He looked with the attribute of His goodness according to the law of His perfection for the sake of these creatures, to rectify them with the complete rectification destined to come, for which He overturns the entire wheel to draw matters of good and evil to perfect completion by the power of His unified dominion.

Soul: I am settled, for the way of general rectification is certainly from the law of His goodness, even as He acts with us only according to our proportion and not His own.

Intellect: Let me inform you of something more particular in this - that in every attribute God measures to us, we discern the revealed and the concealed. The revealed is the reward and punishment meted out according to the attribute, whether good or bad. The concealed is the profound counsel always present in all His attributes to bring creatures to general rectification. For such is the attribute - there is no deed, small or great, whose inner intention is not for complete rectification, as they said (Berachot 60b), "Everything they do from heaven is good." These are the words of the prophet (Isaiah 12:1), "Your anger will turn away and You will comfort me," for God will make known His ways in the future, showing how even rebukes and sufferings were preparations for good and blessing. The Holy One wants only the rectification of His creation and does not reject the wicked, but refines them in the crucible to be cleansed of dross. This single intention is present in all His deeds, to the right and left, as we explained.

You should know that every deed of the Lord is awesome, wide and deep without end, as it is said (Psalms 92:6), "How great are Your works, O Lord"; the smallest deed contains such profound wisdom that its depth cannot be fathomed, as the verse states

(Ibid.), "Your thoughts are very deep." The deeds of the Lord are not understood by us at all, only their superficiality is visible while their true inwardness is concealed. The inside is equal in all of them - they are all only good and not bad at all, though this is certainly not visible and understood now. But in the future, we will at least see and comprehend how they were causes of His profound stratagems to do us good in the end. Let us not imagine that we will comprehend the end of the great wisdom in those deeds, for all that man comprehends of the Creator's works is like a drop from the sea. We will know that since the Master wanted to look with the law of His goodness upon His creatures, all the deeds that reach us now according to reward and punishment have in their midst what is not on their outside - what He always overturns and causes in His goodness to complete our rectification.

There is in this inside what will be revealed in the future, as it is said (Isaiah 35:5), "Then the eyes of the blind shall be opened," referring to the visible intention from the deeds themselves, which we will understand as soon as our eyes are enlightened with knowledge. But there certainly is profound wisdom in those deeds beyond what is recognizable from their effects, due to the loftiness of supreme wisdom. Both of these are the deeds of His goodness that look upon us for good, always according to our proportion and not His, as we explained - following from the law of His perfection, but doing His deeds only as pertains to us. Soul: Summarize this matter as well.

Intellect: This is the rule - God's perfection from His own perspective is not comprehensible at all. But when He wants to act with the law of His goodness, in deeds according to our proportion, He placed counsels and cycles of conduct to bring all creatures to perfection and rectification - this is the concealed, equal side in all His deeds. A small part of this concealment is revealed and recognizable from the deeds themselves when God chooses to open our eyes. However, most of it remains lofty, exalted and incomprehensible due to the depth of His wondrous wisdom.

You need to know that the conduct truly related to the blessed Master is the conduct of perfection, for He is perfect, acting in His perfection. Since He arranged the laws and orders of what reaches creatures according to good and evil, the consequences of those laws and attributes are considered as coming automatically, based on what was decreed in each attribute. Indeed, as long as the conduct of good and evil needs to serve, the actions coming from the laws of good and evil will be drawn from perfection itself, because the source of everything is perfection. Even what is done according to good and evil is a cycle and wheel going toward perfection, but as long as unity is concealed, matters need to go according to this order. Therefore, those actions will automatically be drawn from perfection itself, since according to the supreme will and wisdom they need to emerge from the source of perfection as long as unity is concealed. In the end, the fruit of the action of perfection will be to return the entire conduct to Him completely...This is a third matter to discern in each of His attributes - the drawing of the consequences of that attribute from the power of the action of perfection itself, an intermediary between perfection and the attribute according to its matter, changing in each attribute based on the change of the matter of the attribute, for it is affected by perfection according to its matter. One should discern in this intermediary its essential matter and the way it is done, as we will explain.

We still need to know that all these matters depend only on His will, for they have no existence, being or sustenance except by His will which rules with infinite ability, for He spoke and it was, commanded and it stood fast. The power of His will is known in all of them, for He alone sustains them in all their matters, parts and details, just as He alone sustains all creatures in all their dispositions and all that is in them, for they have no existence besides Him.

Soul: This is simple to me and I have no doubt about it.

Intellect: I will explain further this premise, and you will understand a profound matter and their saying (Genesis Rabbah 68:9), "He is the place of the world and the world is not His place."

Nothing is necessary of existence except His existence, and all else has no existence except by His will, depending on and standing only by His will. All existence depends on His utterance, like what they said about the upper waters (Genesis Rabbah 4:3; Ta'anit 10a) and "On what does the earth stand - on the pillars etc., and the storm hangs on the arm of the Holy One, blessed be He." They further said (Yalkut Shimoni, Part 1, 664), "Flesh and blood is below its load, but the Holy One, blessed be He, is above His load, as it is said (Deuteronomy 33:27), 'Underneath are the everlasting arms,'" comparing Him to one who supports all existence in all its details, standing above them.

The general matter is what I spoke - since the existence innovated by Him is not necessary to Him at all, it is supported only by His simple will. Only His will and decree is the place for all existents; besides this there would be no place at all. Therefore He is certainly eternal, but His creation is not eternal, excluding the heretics who say the world must be eternal since He is. For until He wanted and decreed this, there was no place for creatures to exist; according to His existence they have no matter, for they are not imprinted in the law of a person's nature. He alone must exist necessarily and nothing else - this is simple. But when He wanted them and decreed they should exist, then they have a place, and not without this. When He decreed this, He gave place to all the buildings He built afterwards.

You will further understand that even though we know God rejoices over all His works and they are for His honor, as it is said (Psalms 104:31), "May the glory of the Lord endure for ever; let the Lord rejoice in His works," we should not think that when these did not exist, joy or honor were lacking from Him. We have already said, the blessed Master in His simple existence -

there is no place for creatures with Him at all, for they are not relevant to His matter. But when He wants them, because of this desire and will they exist for Him for joy and honor. This desire gives existence to these existents, and it is not complete if their existence is not done. This is like a place that stands to be built upon, a void until filled with those buildings. Not only the creatures, but all the ways of conduct, laws, and kinds of bestowal according to our proportion and not His have no matter at all except when He wants the existence of the existents. Only according to this desire did He innovate them all; they are not necessary in Him, but are included in the buildings that fill this place, for both are necessary for the completion of this desire. This is simple. We have explained what is sufficient for us in this matter.

Soul: In this matter you have settled me completely. Now I would like to understand the existence of man, for this is what needs to be properly understood, as all inquiries revolve around him and the burden of service is upon him.

Intellect: You are right - man is the ultimate purpose in all God's deeds. Only one who understands this clearly will know the essence of all that precedes it, for the aim of everything is to come to this purpose.

Soul: Even here we will have to inquire very much.

Intellect: We need to speak of three things - the existence of man, his deeds, and the fruit of his deeds.

Soul: If so, the inquiry is exceedingly broad.

Intellect: But we will say the beginning of words, and leave the rest of the explanation to the wise, who will become wiser.

Soul: Speak your words.

Intellect: Here we need to come to the matter of the resurrection of the dead, which we certainly believe in without any doubt.
The matter of the resurrection is simple in brief and in general. When the Holy One created man, body and soul, to serve and carry out the service of holiness, the Torah and commandments He gave them, it is fitting that they should also receive the eternal reward together. It is not proper that the body should labor and not be rewarded, for God does not withhold the reward of any creature (Bava Kamma 38b). But what needs contemplation is the details of this connection of body and soul - in their connection, separation, and return to complete connection, for the Almighty does all these things with every man, and it is certainly not in vain. These details require broad and sufficient explanation.

Soul: This matter certainly needs explanation. Why did God make body and soul in two creations and not one, that man should be one existence without being composed as he is now? It is not beyond Him to make man alive in himself, without this division of body and Soul. I think that when we know this, it will be an open door to enter the rest of the details.

Intellect: The supreme intention, as you have heard, is to benefit man, to let him merit in his deeds what will rectify and complete his creation. This is the matter of deficiency and perfection we mentioned. God made this body a thick, dark matter, unfit for the light of His holiness to shine in it due to its lowly species, for only the perfect in preparation may come to the gate of the king and visit his palace, all the more so from the earthly kingdom. This darkness imprinted in the body's law is what places in it all the evil lusts that rule over it, making it susceptible to all the evil accidents that befall it.

Second - He made the pure soul, hewn from under the throne of glory, and brought it down to breathe into this body to purify and sanctify it. This needs to be understood, for the end of the intention in the soul's coming into the body is not just to enliven it with these fleeting lives, but to refine it, elevating it from the lowly level of its material darkness to the supreme level, like the ministering angels. We have found this in Moshe, who merited and refined his materiality until he returned to the level of an actual angel, and all Israel saw that his face shone (Exodus 34:29-30). Enoch and Elijah ascended to heaven in their actual bodies, after greatly refining their materiality (Genesis 5:24; II Kings 2:11).

The way the soul can refine its body is through the performance of the commandments and observance of the Torah, the lamp and light (Proverbs 6:23). The more it increases Torah and commandments, the more refinement it increases for the body, and merit for itself in fulfilling its Maker's will.

Soul: We have found complete benefit for the body, and merit for the soul, but not complete benefit for the soul.

Intellect: We will still speak of this with God's help. Let us complete our subject. This refinement is the main action of the soul in this world; afterwards it has other matters, which this is not the place to explain. On this they said (Zohar, Part 1, Midrash Hane'elam, 115a), "As long as the body stands in this world, it is lacking in completeness; after it is righteous and has gone in the ways of uprightness and has died in its uprightness - it is called lacking in its completeness." This is the fruit of its righteousness - the exaltation of the honor of the omnipresent, Who is exalted in the perfection of His creatures, for He created everything for His honor (Isaiah 43:7). This is all that will be born from the good deed toward above, for which a reward is established, for like the gratification it made before Him, so will He do for it.

But sin causes the sin of Adam to pass the cup of death over all creatures, leaving no hope. The soul cannot make this refinement before death - this is the righteous who died because of the serpent's incitement, who could not be perfected even with their many deeds without this (Bava Batra 17a). But after the dust returns to the earth and the contamination the serpent injected into Eve completely ceases, when the body is rebuilt, the soul will descend into it with all the force of its good deeds and the radiance of the supreme light it enjoys in the Garden of Eden according to its deeds. It will illuminate the body with a great light, completely refining it, recovering from all the evils to which it was susceptible at first. This was explained in the Midrash Hane'elam, Parashat Vayera (Zohar, Part 1, 116a): "Our Sages said - the soul, while in its level is nourished by the light from above and clothed in it, and when it enters the body in the future - it will enter with that very light," and further, "The Holy One puts this body under the earth until it completely rots, and all the evil contamination comes out of it."

We now have the matter of man's service and receiving his reward - the two times that include all his existence. Now in this world, the body is coarse and dark with deficiencies, and the soul has to overcome it with illumination and holiness to refine and make it shine. When this refinement is completed, it is the time of receiving the reward, for they will be together to receive a good reward for all days.

What needs to be understood is the measure of the soul's power given to it to stand within this body. If its power and light were very great, it would give such illumination to the body that it would be elevated and its deficiencies perfected in one moment. The evil inclination - the main deficiency the blessed Master wanted for choice, reward and punishment - would not rule over man at all, as it does not rule over the angels due to their great illumination and perfection of knowledge (Sanhedrin 93b). In the future it is said (Isaiah 11:9), "They shall not hurt nor destroy in all My holy mountain; for the earth shall be full of the knowledge," and (Ezekiel 36:26) "I will take away the stony heart out of your flesh," because of the great level the soul will grow to. But if the soul were essentially low and not great, it would not be able to withstand the preciousness and greatness done to it in the future, to be more than the ministering angels.

The matter is that the soul in its existence and root is very great, but to come into this body, the Holy One diminishes its light and power, leaving it only the measure fitting for the body in this world. At that time it is like the moon of which it is said (Chullin 60b), "Go and diminish yourself," and in the future (Isaiah 30:26), "The light of the moon shall be as the light of the sun." It has good in its hand - to be elevated from exaltation to exaltation up to its supreme force, according to the perfection of its deeds. According to the diminution of power given to it in this world, it stands closed and locked within this opaque body all its days, to be tested in the trials of the evil inclination, placed in man for this purpose, as our Sages said (Zohar, Part 1, 106b), "The evil inclination was created only to test the children of men with it." According to the aptitude of its deeds, it merits an exaltation, elevated from level to level. At the time of reward, all souls find their action with them, exalted in their level according to their deeds. In this level they will return and refine their bodies at the resurrection, delighting in the abundance of peace forever, as we explained above.

Intellect: It follows for us that the soul needs to have a great root from its own perspective, and its source needs to be very honorable, so it will be worthy of all the honor it will have in the future. But they lower it, to elevate and better it in the end, by the blessed Master placing upon it His law, saying, "Go and diminish yourself," to enter this opaque body and be in it all the days of its fleeting life. There He placed for it a law and judgment - this entire Torah to serve and keep (Genesis 2:15), which pertain to it while in this body. But because its great power has weakened and its great light has dimmed in this diminishment, the body remains opaque as it is this day, even with the soul within it. According to the righteousness of its deeds, it is judged for the future, being elevated in the exaltation of its levels. When it comes a second time into the body with that new light, it will do what it cannot do now - completely refine the body, returning it to an honorable and clear essence, as we explained. For at first, to come into the body, the soul needed to diminish its light; but in this second coming, it has to come with all light, to make the refinement completely as it should.

There is a benefit for the soul itself in perfecting the body - to be elevated from exaltation to exaltation, adding power to power and honor to honor. And not only this, but even while in this world within the body, it has exaltation and superiority according to its deeds. A person's soul who engaged in Torah and commandments and attained knowledge in the honor of its Maker is not similar to a soul lacking in all these. But its exaltation does not reach the point of changing the body, so its refinement is visible to the eyes, except in a few, the remnants whom the Lord has chosen, like Moshe, Enoch and Elijah (Exodus 34:29-30; Genesis 5:24; II Kings 2:11). Besides them, even as it attains superiority from its deeds, it does not reach the level of being seen in the body. But good will not be withheld from its owners in the future (Psalms 84:12), each according to his deeds.

Soul: Gather the principle from all that you have said.

Intellect: This is the principle - the body's creation is dark and with deficiencies, and it has refinement through the soul. The soul's source is great, but it diminishes itself when it comes into the body, so it will not greatly increase its refinement all at once and change it from its creation, but little by little it will effect what is necessary through good deeds. Afterwards it will be elevated in exaltations according to its deeds, its power growing according to its exaltation, increasing the refinement in the body according to the greatness of its power, until it will be worthy to stand with it together to behold the pleasantness of the Lord and visit His temple, forever and for all eternity (Psalms 27:4).

Soul: I have understood what is sufficient for me now regarding the resurrection and future reward. Now we need to complete the matters we began with.

The Creation of Evil and its Boundaries

Intellect: After knowing the existence of man and his matter, both in soul and body, in the change of times and order of times decreed for him, we need to understand how the Holy One conducts Himself with him in all these times, both for his body and soul.

Soul: The order is certainly proper, for everything needs to be settled on its wheels in its place and time. Now please complete your words.

Intellect: We have already explained that three matters need to be discerned in every conduct of the blessed Master. The first is the matter of perfection itself. The second is the attribute and law evident from that conduct. The third is the drawing of the consequences of that attribute from the power of the action of perfection, an intermediary between perfection and the attribute according to its matter.

The way of providence toward man also includes all these three matters. At the beginning, the Master in His perfection prepared and established man in the most complete manner, with no deficiency at all, as it is written (Genesis 1:31), "And God saw every thing that He had made, and it was very good." Our Sages said (Genesis Rabbah 9:5), "'Very good' refers to the evil inclination," for even it was very good and necessary for the complete good, being the material of the service of choice for which man was created, as our Sages said (Ecclesiastes Rabbah 3:11), "It would have been better for man not to have been created than to have been created, but now that he has been created, let him examine his deeds." This is what they said - that he should constantly examine his deeds and choose good, for this is his complete perfection.

But as we explained above, since the Master wanted man to attain his perfection through his choice and deeds, He had to make the order of good and evil in the world, and place man between them to choose as he wishes and receive according to his choice. Here the second matter is already evident - the attribute and law, which are the laws of reward and punishment, good and evil. This had to be innovated in providence, so there would be a place for choice and deeds, to be with merit as we mentioned. Therefore the blessed Master had to hide His countenance of eternal life, so there would be a place for the created beings to die if they corrupted their ways and rebelled against their Master, since this death is what they chose for themselves of their own will, as explained above. This itself is their judgment - that their will is fulfilled in them.

The third matter is already explained - that from the power of the action of perfection itself, the drawing of the orders of providence had to come out, for it prepared a cure before the blow. From the perspective of the action of perfection, everything was prepared to return to it. Therefore, those consequences of good and evil and conducts of providence have to be drawn from perfection itself, to return to it, for this is its perfection. For this reason, death which came into the world because of the sin of Adam who ate from the Tree of

Knowledge, perfection itself turned it into an opening and preparation for all the perfections destined to emerge in the future. For if not for death, man's body would not be rebuilt in the manner explained above (76). Everything is included in that sin, which is the sin of the evil choice. Therefore, according to the laws of choice, there must be complete corruption for the sinners, as explained above, and this is the rule for all sins. But Divine perfection prepared, through this itself, every goodness mentioned above, to give good to the righteous and also to the sinners who corrupted their way at first but then repented and corrected their deeds, and to grant them life from the dead, an eternal and perfect life.

Soul: I am amazed by this, for how can the evil deeds make preparation for such good? But now I will not ask about this, for I know that according to what you have prefaced, there will certainly be a way to understand it. So please continue.

Intellect: The sin is certainly not the preparation for the good, but the death that comes because of it is the preparation. For the death and evil of the wicked is what necessitates at first to make a preparation so that he will not die and be lost. But in the end, when he dies, that death makes it possible to renew him again. If not for that death, there would be no place for his renewal. But the ways of God are very deep, and now is not the place to elaborate on this. When the time comes for this, with God's help, it will be explained well.

The General Providence Toward Man

Intellect: Now, let us return to complete our first subject. We need to understand the general providence toward man in his body and soul, in his life and in his death, in his choice and in his deeds, in his reward and in his punishment - how does the Blessed One conduct it, and what is the matter conducted according to His attributes of perfection?

Soul: In your words you have given a general answer to every detail, that everything is included in the three manners mentioned above. But now we need the details in their place, and especially I desire to hear the details of providence in the matter of man's choice, which is the main part of his merit and iniquity.

Intellect: Indeed, choice is an exceedingly deep matter. But the general principle is simple, as the faithful shepherd said (Deuteronomy 30:19), "I call heaven and earth to witness against you this day, that I have set before you life and death, the blessing and the curse; therefore choose life." Before your eyes it is stated that the Holy One, Blessed be He, has placed before man free choice. As our Sages said (Sifrei there), "The matter is given over to the heart of each man; if he wants to incline himself to the path of life he may do so, and if he wants to incline himself to the path of death he may do so." For this is certainly the foundation for the commandments and the prohibitions, as they said (Genesis Rabbah 34:10), "Why was man created alone? So that the heretics should not say there are many domains in Heaven. Another answer: For the sake of the righteous and the wicked, so that the righteous should not say, 'We are the children of a righteous man,' and the wicked should not say, 'We are the children of a wicked man.'" They said further (Niddah 16b), "Everything is in the hands of Heaven except for the fear of Heaven, as it is stated: 'And now Israel, what does the Lord your God ask of you, only to fear etc.'(Deuteronomy 10:12)."

However, the ways of the Holy One, Blessed be He, are deep and hidden. Even though He gave man free choice, He also prepared causes to assist him in his choice. As they said (Shabbat 104a), "One who comes to purify himself is assisted." Conversely, sometimes He prepares things that damage his choice, as in the case of Pharaoh. As they said (Exodus Rabbah 13:3), "The Holy One, Blessed be He, warns a person once, twice, and three times, and if he still does not repent, He closes his heart against repentance in order to punish him for his sins." These ways are hidden and secretive, and the human intellect cannot comprehend them in an orderly manner. This is the meaning of (Isaiah 55:8), "For My thoughts are not your thoughts and your ways are not My ways."

Soul: If so, what is the power of choice? And what is the praise of the righteous and the reproach of the wicked? For if matters are prepared for a person to assist him or to damage him, his choice is coerced and he is not free!

Intellect: But you already know that the Holy One, Blessed be He, knows everything that will happen in the future, and before Him everything is revealed and known. As they said (Pirkei Avot 3:15), "Everything is foreseen." If we understand this, the difficulty will be resolved. For the Holy One, Blessed be He, knows in advance who will choose good and who will choose evil, and based on this, Divine providence is directed. Before the righteous one even begins the act, he is already prepared and assisted.

But the wicked one is the opposite; he is stricken because of his wickedness that is yet to come. But if he repents, then he too is treated accordingly, as in (Ezekiel 33:12), "The wickedness of the wicked shall not cause him to stumble when he repents of his wickedness." For the knowledge of the Holy One, Blessed be He, does not force man's choice at all, since it is knowledge that does not depend on cause and effect. On the contrary, the choice precedes the knowledge, for if there were no free choice, foreknowledge would have no basis at all.

Soul: These words make sense, but I still do not understand - if everything is revealed and known before Him, how is it possible for man to choose freely? For he is compelled to do what the Almighty already knows!

Intellect: But you forgot the great, important fundamental that we already explained above (40), that the Holy One, Blessed be He, limited Himself, as it were. He acted toward His creations not according to the laws of His own truth, but according to what was necessary for the creations. His knowledge is not at all a cause for the known things, since if so, His knowledge would force them to exist as He knows them. But the Holy One, Blessed be He, in His supreme kindness, arranged for Himself not to do so, but to allow created things to have their own nature, and for man to have actual free choice. Therefore, His knowledge does not compel anything, but only follows the facts. Man's choice itself determines the facts, and Divine knowledge follows it. This is the depth of (Pirkei Avot 3:15), "Everything is foreseen, and free choice is given." Even though everything is foreseen, free choice remains in full force.

Soul: Even though this is a very deep concept, it is sweet to my palate as I contemplate it. Please continue to explain this matter thoroughly.

Intellect: See, there are physical entities and spiritual entities. You see how much difference there is between these and those, for physicality is certainly inferiority compared to spirituality, whose matter is honorable and superior. You see how much illumination there is in the spiritual ones and how much darkness and deficiency there is in the physical ones. We have here two types of creation - a creation with great illumination and expansive influence, and a creation with little illumination and little influence. These two attributes - the attribute of creation with illumination and the attribute of creation without illumination - the attribute of illumination is from the descendants of the rule of His goodness, and the attribute of creation without illumination from the descendants of the concealment of His goodness.

You will see that the spiritual ones - all their engagement is in matters of holiness; but the physical ones - their matters are secular, lowly and despicable things. It turns out that all of man's toil under the sun is nothing but vanity of vanities, and man's superiority over beasts is nothing for eating and drinking (Ecclesiastes 1:2; 3:19), and they will trade the earth, for all these are certainly inferior and light matters. In sum, all matters of physicality and this nature are darkness and not light, for the Lord hides His face from the world and does not illuminate it with the illumination of His holiness; on the contrary, He leads in futility not in the way, in these lowly ways.

But the matters of the spiritual ones - this is the way the light of His countenance will dwell, for He illuminates them with His holiness, and this is simple. You shall know now that these two are the foundations of His guidance and its root with all His creatures - the attribute of concealment of the face, that He conceals and hides and does not reveal the splendor of His glory, and the attribute of illumination of the face.

The Concealment and Illumination of God's Face

Intellect: What is in the guidance is in the creation, for the coarse, opaque creatures were only created with the concealment of the face, for He did not shine His holy face upon them, and the honorable spiritual ones are created with the illumination of the face. On the basis of these foundations, this combination of body and soul was made; for the body, its matters in all their ways, are drawn and come in the concealment of the face; and the soul and all its matters - in the illumination of the face. Man himself is the repairer and the one being repaired, for he repairs himself with his service, and this is the matter of (Sanhedrin 99b), "And you shall do them" - "and you shall do them" is written, which our Sages expounded. It is in his hand to strengthen in himself the physicality and its ways, or the spirituality and its ways. For if he follows the sight of his eyes and the physical ways of his heart, behold his soul, instead of benefitting this body and purifying it as we explained, on the contrary, causes great harm and damage to itself, for it sinks into darkness. The opposite of this, if he overcomes his inclination and turns away from the ways of futility, to walk in the ways of the Torah and the commandment - the soul will overcome the body and purify it.

Now you will see the cycle of the world, and what is between the early generations and the later generations. In truth, one who takes this matter to heart, that God gave to be occupied with, will be very amazed at the desire to see people running to and from, day and night they do not cease, each to his own way weary and tired. Why do they toil - for eating and drinking, for futility of futilities that is nothing, for a world of chaos that was between night, today here and tomorrow in the grave. But one who will look well will see and understand that man was not created for this, but it would have been fitting for his occupation to be only in attaining the glory of his Maker, for this is why he was created, and intellect and great wisdom were placed in him, and not to increase in commerce, or all other insignificant things.

But man is the one who corrupted his deeds, and caused himself these things today. In each and every generation the world becomes more and more lacking in this matter. For the early ones were closer to wisdom, and ascended to the intellect, and the later ones are further from the intellect, and sink into the matters of physicality and this nature, in commerce and in all the thought of craft, which man will not find anything after him, and as we explained above. The root of all this is what we said, that the Unique Master, blessed be He, created the body with the concealment of the face, and not with the illumination of the face, therefore its existence was dark and opaque; this is not so for the soul, for it, on the contrary, is created with the illumination of the face and with a view to goodness, therefore it is eternal and everlasting, and its creation is pure. However, if man empowers his body and gives it dominion, behold the Master, may He be blessed, with the measure that he measures so will He measure to him - to guide him only with the concealment of the face. From here it turns out that he will be far from the light of life, from wisdom and knowledge, and immersed in the dung of the impurity of materialism and the vanities of this world.

You will see that this is what happened to man from the beginning, and to his offspring after him as of this day; for since they followed their eyes, and gave dominion to the body and not the soul, therefore the Holy One, Blessed be He, also went with them in the concealment of the face. To man He said from the beginning, "By the sweat of your brow you shall eat bread" (Genesis 3:19), and from that day onward "All of man's toil is for his mouth, yet his soul is not satisfied" (Ecclesiastes 6:7). Wisdom continually went and departed from mankind.

This is a great principle - in the boundary in which his intellect is bounded, so are the thoughts of man and his lusts. You see, the young child does not recognize what wisdom is, and does not desire it at all, but on the contrary, every child runs away from school, and does not think that there is good except in the vanities with which he occupies himself; and with the increase of his knowledge and the expansion of his boundary, he will return to desire more proper things, and in this way according to all his elevation. So it is for humanity as a whole - when their intellect was influenced by great illumination, they found no contentment except from wisdom, and from what is truly good; and when their intellect is not influenced, they recognize nothing as good except the vanities of this earth. This is the evil that was done after the sin of Adam, that the influence and illumination were removed from the human race, and they remained immersed only in the matters of coarse materialism.

However, the Holy One, Blessed be He, remedied for Israel with the giving of the Torah, but they corrupted for themselves with the calf and all their other transgressions for all their sins, and the world remained in darkness in the imagined ways of nature. Not so when man gives dominion to his soul, for then the Holy One, Blessed be He, will also shine His countenance upon him, and elevate him to a great elevation to be like one of the Seraphim, for the righteous are greater than the ministering angels (Sanhedrin 93a), and as was for the generation of knowledge on Mount Sinai, and as will be in the future in the time when it is said (Joel 3:1), "I will pour out My spirit upon all flesh" etc.

Even in this good there are levels that Israel and the world merited in different generations, sometimes more and sometimes less; for example, the generation of Moshe, the generation of David, the generation of Solomon, and likewise all the generations that merited goodness, it was all the illumination of His countenance, upon them according to the elevation of their soul, which they elevated with the power of their deeds.

See, that when we understand the details of the existence of the body and the soul, and their states in the concealment of the face and in the illumination of the face, as they were created in all the distinctions of their details in this matter, we will consequently understand the general orders of His guidance, that He guided and that He guides His world, sometimes for good and sometimes for bad, God forbid; and we will see how much great wisdom we find in this guidance; and we will also see how great a principle is man, that in him - in his matter and in his deeds - the entire world depends, and all that is done in it from beginning to end.

Soul: Certainly these matters are very well settled in the heart, to see great wisdom in His guidances, and how the matters are connected to each other - the creation of man and all his occurrences, the creation of the world and all that is in it.

Intellect: I will say more to you in this matter, that when we descend to the details of the matters of the soul and the body, we will well understand how they are all dependent on this root of these two attributes that we mentioned, for each of them is judged in all its matters according to its source, and this will be a sufficient reason for all these matters. Moreover, it was the decree of the Supreme Wisdom to show the ways of these attributes in this body and soul that come through them. We find that apart from the body coming in the concealment of the face, it and its matters, it itself in its nature and parts is also a depiction of the guidance of the entire concealment of the face; and the soul too is a depiction of the entire guidance of the illumination of the face. This is a particular matter for the image of this man of whom it is said (Genesis 1:26), "In our image, after our likeness" - that it shows in its form all the orders of His attributes.

You will see that the existence of the body is only dark, for even if it reaches the greatest merit that can be found in it, in any case it must be separated from the soul, and it is only separated by this difference - that the soul is an honorable illuminating entity and comes from the illumination of His countenance, and the body is not so, but rather a thing that is intrinsically dark, coming from the concealment of His countenance, except that purification will fall upon it to the place it can reach, and that is to the last end that there will be a small difference between it and the soul. But in any case, the soul will be a soul - a thing in which no harm is applicable at all; and the body, on the contrary - a thing that is destructible by its nature, except that it reached to be purified in the purification it reached.

You will see further, that the body indeed has distinctions of organs and parts, each for its function, for the eye sees and does not hear, and the ear hears and does not see; this is not so for the soul, for it has all the powers, but without the distinction of these organs like the organs of the body, but all of it is in every part, and this is known. Now you will see how this follows well from the premise we set, that the body was created in the concealment of the face and the soul in the illumination of the face. You will see a great and very fundamental premise - you have already heard that perfection is one, for no lack or excess is applicable in true perfection. But when the Holy One, Blessed be He, does not want to act in His perfection, then there are many ways for the Place to reward or punish, each according to his deeds, and as we explained above.

Since it was the decree of the Supreme Wisdom to show in the creation itself the order and way how He created it, as we explained, therefore in the concealment of the face - just as His ways are many, so did He want to make this creation of His with many parts and different organs, that they should correspond precisely to all the parts of His laws.

This is the matter that I mentioned to you, that of this it is said, "Let us make man in our image, after our likeness," for in all the excellent attributes by which His glory, is discerned, in His acting according to the level of His creatures, so are parts found in the form of this man; for example, an eye - corresponding to the eye of His supervision that oversees all the inhabitants of the earth to judge all their deeds, as it is stated (Genesis 18:21), "I will go down now and see" - to teach you that a judge has only what his eyes see (Sanhedrin 6b). Ears for man - corresponding to the Holy One, Blessed be He, sitting and listening to the prayers of human beings and all their praises, and so it is said (Exodus 2:24), "And God heard their groaning"; and our Sages said (Avot 2:1), "Know what is above you - a seeing eye and a hearing ear." A mouth in man - for the mouth of the Lord spoke in a vision to His prophets, and proclaims the majesty of His voice to His mighty angels who perform His word.

So all similar to this, all the other parts of the body are all well explained, their forms and matters corresponding to His attributes, which He prepared to act upon His creatures. Man's body is made right and left, with its matters doubled here and there, two eyes, two ears, two hands, two feet, just as His attribute, is also double - whether for kindness or for His rod, to the right for merit or to the left for liability. This is the way that the Supreme Will took after concealing His perfection that equates everything to good. Indeed, just as these parts of the body are discerned and distinguished so according to their function, so all the occurrences of man in the concealment of the face are causes that are reversed in His schemes to activate them, like all that we see in the children of time, the matter of each and every day.

But perfection, as I have already said, is one, to dominate over all the lack to complete it, and it does not divide in itself, but in one equation it completes all who need completion. So is this matter in the soul created in the illumination of the countenance of this perfection. You will see that this is indeed the intention - to empower the soul over the body and to purify it, so that the Almighty, may He be blessed, will also measure to it as its deed, to be also He revealing His perfection, to repair every perversion and every deficiency in the world, and as we explained above. The body is prepared for punishment when it has ruled in man, for so the Holy One, Blessed be He, will conceal the countenance of His perfection, and guide it with heaviness, under the laws of the revolving orb in all its circumstances, like the law of all transient beings upon whom the times change to all the directions it turns.

Therefore, there is in the body all that is fitting to be found in the order of the revolving orb in the world, in the concealment of the perfection of the good, in order to arouse upon it all these, if only it has the kingship in man, that it should rule over him. There is in the soul that which is fitting for perfection, to complete every deficiency, in order to arouse upon it the like if man will merit his path, and the crown of kingship is placed on its head, to be it alone ruling in its wisdom and the law of its reason, for it is good.

Indeed, they explained this matter well in the Midrash of Rabbi Shimon bar Yochai (Zohar, Pinchas 257b), may his memory be for a blessing, "And one must know that He is called wise in all kinds of wisdom," for besides what the knowers of truth explained it according to their holy ways, behold from the simple meaning of the teaching we learned what I already explained to you above, that the Holy One, Blessed be He, has many appellations, not according to Himself but according to His creatures, and this is what they said (ibid.), "According to the name of the creatures that were destined to be created."
Indeed they said "according to the name of the creatures" is simple, for we do not say that it is something that was innovated in Him, God forbid, for there is no innovation and change in Him, but also initially it was in His power to do this, but these attributes are always only what is relevant to His creatures, not what is relevant to Himself. He said, "In this way He created the soul," and this is the fact that the existence of the soul shows His perfection, in which it was created; "So too the Master of the world etc., but all the names are His like the manner of the Sefirot etc., and just as the Master of the world has no known name etc., so too the soul has no known name" etc., see there. You must examine this matter well in order to understand the existence of the body and the soul properly, and all that depends on this.

The Unique Master, according to His perfection it is impossible to give Him any name or appellation, because we do not comprehend His perfection, and it is impossible to give a name to that which one does not comprehend, for the name is a definition of the bearer of the name, and that which one does not know with complete knowledge - it is impossible to define it. Indeed we comprehend in His glory, particular attributes, such as mercy, dominion, power, justice, compassion, anger, strength, and the like, all the attributes that we comprehend in Him - they are from the perspective of His actions, those attributes that the prophets comprehend in Him from the prior to the posterior, because He, may He be blessed, gives them this comprehension. According to this comprehension that we have comprehended in His glory, we call Him, with these appellations - merciful, ruler, mighty, judge, and the like.

Even though He, may He be blessed, in His perfection is without boundary and measure at all, but these attributes that He wanted, He wanted them with the boundary and measure that He wanted; and therefore, one attribute is called mercy, and another - dominion, and one attribute - power, and one attribute - love, and so all of them. There is nothing in the attribute of mercy but mercy, and not in dominion except dominion, and also in mercy there is only that measure that He, may He be blessed, wants in it, and not in dominion but the measure that He wants in it, and so all of them. We will not say because of this that He, may He be blessed, according to His perfection has these powers in these measures, but all this depends on His will, and as we explained, that He is the Master to change all this; and on the contrary, in His perfection we have no estimation of any measure at all.

However, because He wants to grasp these attributes, and to act in this way, therefore we relate these appellations to Him.

We will not understand when we call the Holy One, Blessed be He, merciful, to say that His essence, according to Himself is so, as we would say about a person who has this nature in his soul to be merciful - that so is imprinted in his temperament, that His matter should be grasped and comprehended from Him in any way, God forbid, for this we must not think at all, for it is impossible to know of His matter, what He is according to Himself in truth at all. But when we call Him merciful, we will understand that He wants one attribute, which is the attribute of mercy, an attribute that is not according to Himself, but rather according to the level of the creatures, and measured in their measure. But because He wants this, and He grasps this way, we call Him by this name - merciful. But His perfect and simple essence is certainly outside all these matters. This is the faith that we are obligated to believe in Him, may He be blessed, certainly, and as we have already explained this above.

Now we will understand this very matter in body and soul. For the body has individual parts and organs, with particular limited functions; but the soul, According to itself it is one matter, completely outside all matters of the body, and all its ways are other ways, different from the ways of the body in every respect, even in the matters of the senses themselves. But because it is the one that does all the deeds of the body when it is within it, it is the one that hears with the ears of the body, it is the one that sees with the eyes of the body, and so all similar to this, therefore it is called - seeing, hearing, and all the other appellations; but not that it has these ways at all.

For even though the soul alone is the one that sees, and not the body which is inanimate, and it turns out that it is the one that sees things as people in their perfection truly see; this is not its way of sight at all, for it has another way that is completely different from any way of the functions of the body, and it is a way that man cannot estimate while he is in his body. But because it is the one that grasps the law of that eye to see according to the law engraved in it, therefore it is said that it is the one that sees, and so all the other functions. But the principle is that the soul is one created kind far in its matter from all the ways of the body completely, but it was created with its law to do all that is rooted in the organs of the body according to their nature.

Behold, it grasps these laws, and does in the body all these deeds, therefore they are all related to it. This is precisely like the matter of His perfection, in relation to the particular attributes that He wanted, for perfection has no matter at all from these attributes, but these are particular attributes that He wanted, limited and measured in the measure that He wanted them. But because He, may He be blessed - the Perfect One in His perfection - is the One who acts according to these attributes, therefore we call Him by these names and appellations, and relate these acts and descriptions to Him, even though He in His perfection is truly simple in all these matters, and has no relation on His part with any one of these ways and these acts at all.

Soul: This is indeed the correspondence explained between both the body and the soul, and it is a great gate that is opened to understand all the matters of man in all his times.

Intellect: We still need to come to the gradation of the times of the soul and the body, and these their different states. But one more premise needs to be put forth first, and that is, that it is simple that many laws and many ways are needed in order to complete all the matters of man, and all the matters of creation in all their times; and it has already been said (Psalms 40:6), "Many things you have done, O Lord my God, your wonders and your thoughts" etc., and it is said (Psalms 92:6), "How great are your works, O Lord," (Psalms 104:24), "How many are your works, O Lord" etc. But in any case, the details must enter and come under the generalizations, and the generalizations will not be so many, but their details are what will be many, and will suffice for all that is needed in this entire creation.

Soul: This is certainly simple, there are no details that do not have generalizations over them, and what the details tire the mind to gather them, the generalizations are amenable to it to receive them. Therefore, generalizations should be pursued, and not details.

Intellect: So our Sages said (Sifrei Ha'azinu 32:2), "The words of Torah should always be in your hand as generalizations and not as details." Let us return to our matter. You have already seen the two attributes of Him, may He be blessed - the concealment of the face and the illumination of the face, they are the root and cause of the body and the soul. We are to understand these two attributes each one by itself, in all their many details included under their generalizations, in order to know the matters of the soul and the body, each one by itself in all their details as well. After we have found and known this, we still have to know that these two attributes come as one to guide the entire world and its inhabitants, and there is nothing that does not have a place for these two attributes - the concealment in revelation, and the illumination in concealment, and as we explained above. After that we will go to understand and comprehend the consequences that come out of the combinations of these two attributes, when one or the other prevails. We have here three types of knowledge - knowledge of the two attributes, this by itself and that by itself; knowledge of their combination to always act together; knowledge of the consequences born of this combination according to their kinds, according to the prevalence in them of concealment or illumination.

Soul: I am pondering after you said that the Holy One, Blessed be He, wanted to show the orders of His creation and its ways in the creation itself, that accordingly these two attributes in which man is guided, in which he was created, are seen in him himself in the two parts of which he is composed and built, and they are, the body and the soul; and this is the matter of the first type of knowledge that you mentioned. Also for the second we have the correspondence explained in man, for the soul indeed combines with the body and spreads into all its parts, to do every act through both of them equally as one. But for the third I will ask of you, is there a correspondence for it? For I have not found it.
Intellect: You will also find a correspondence for this, if you will examine with a deep examination this structure of man. For,

besides the image of the body in its form, and besides the soul that is in it in the form that it has, there is one thing that exists from the combination of both of them - it is the radiance of the face. You will see that this is what distinguishes the living from the dead. Not only this, but even the change of the settling of the soul in the body is seen in it.

You see, the face of the sick is bad; and moreover, even the thought of the heart is seen in it, you see, laughing faces, angry faces, welcoming faces - all of them are their witnesses of the hidden thoughts in the nearness of the heart. This radiance does not exist either for the soul by itself, for it is the radiance of a body, nor for the body by itself, for the body does not have this radiance without the soul; but it is the thing born of the combination of the soul and the body together.

This matter is not an empty thing, for when the prophets compare the form to its Maker, as we explained, when the supreme glory appears to them in His attributes, and rules parables, it is in His showing His attributes to their eyes as a young mighty man for war, or as an old man full of mercy for sitting, and as our Sages said (Chagigah 14a).

Behold, the prophet's eye will imagine, and his heart will think so, to understand in the vision of his prophecy the concealment of His face and the illumination of His goodness, and that which is born of their combinations, like the appearance of a man upon him from above, who has a body and a soul and a radiant face from the combination of both of them together, whether welcoming, or laughing, or angry, to know all that the Lord God will do a thing in His world, to the right or to the left.

The Dominion of the Soul and Body in Different States

Soul: This is enough for me now in this matter for the correspondence. Let us return to the knowledge of the guidance itself in its gradations.

Intellect: This comes out first in the consequences of the combinations of these two attributes as one, the perfect state that is fitting to be for man in the time of the ultimate perfection that will be for him. The matter is clear by itself, that the ultimate level, which will be the end of all man's elevation, it is the one that is fixed first, for from the time the soul emanated from its source it must be in its law the greatest perfection that it can reach at the very end, but they will say to it from above, "Go and diminish yourself," until it returns to its first place in its elevation by its deeds. But not that its creation is diminished at first, and its elevation will be increased after it, for there is nothing new under the sun, but the order is the opposite of this, for with its great power from the time it emanates, afterwards - they will diminish for it, until it returns to its strength. In any case - the end of the deed is the beginning of the thought. Therefore, man's perfection is what is fixed first, and after it - his diminution, to return in the elevations in which he descended, to ascend to his perfection as was engraved for him from the beginning.

It turns out that man's state of perfection is what is discerned first, and it is the way and time that the soul alone will be ruling and reigning completely, without there being any dominion for the body at all, and as if it does not exist, for it is all subjugated and bent completely under the dominion of the soul in its purity, until I do not even mention it by name, since only existence it has, but not dominion. This is simple, for the dominion of the body is only darkness and gloom for the soul, for the matter of physicality is only concealment of illumination, and any of it - hinders, for it is impossible for even a small dominion for the body, that there will not be lacking corresponding to it some light and power from the soul.

Therefore, the time that the soul will be in all its might, that it will not lack anything in it of what is fitting for it for its perfection, it is certainly the time that the body has no dominion, therefore the soul has no hindrance. But do not say that it will not have existence, for we have already said that the reward must be for both of them, but it will not have dominion, and it will all be bound after the soul, not separating from it, for it will not do anything alone, and there will not be in its will anything that will not be in its will, until it will hardly be discerned as a thing in itself, but rather as if it is absorbed among the pure powers of the soul.

A state less than this, is when the body is discerned in its dominion a little, for therefore a deficiency will reach corresponding to this to the soul, not to be perfect in all its glorious splendor; but dominion, however small, will only produce a deficiency, however small, but if the dominion increases then the deficiency will increase. Indeed, if we speak in one generalization only, we will say that there are three times in this - a time of the complete dominion of the soul, and a time of the dominion of the body a little, and a time of the complete dominion of the body. But if we go in the way of gradation, to further understand these states of the body in its dominion - we can count five levels in it in a general way.

Level 1 - it is that the body will have existence, but no dominion at all, until there will not be any hint in the world of the matters of physicality, as there are now. It turns out, that in this state man will not find in himself anything of those things that he has now when his physicality rules over him, and this is the most perfect state of all the states.

Level 2 - that the body will have some dominion, and man will find in himself like a mention of what he had in the time of having a body, and this is not a mention of particular things, but a general mention of many things that were in him. A parable for one who underwent many troubles, and toiled and labored in many adventures, and afterwards there remained exhaustion in him and fatigue in general. For so the existence of the dominion of the body produces one general deficiency, not distinguished what it is in particular, but rather like a man who has some sorrow in his heart, that his joy is not complete, even though there is no particular reason for that sorrow. So the power of the soul will not be found in itself to spread in all its powers, but it will feel like some slight heaviness for it, and the details of the hindrance are not known.

Level 3 - when the body rules in particular, but not in all its details, but only in some of its details. That man will find in himself some things of the matters of the body, the lightest things, but in any case physical. Indeed it is simple, that in all these states there are no great consequences for these matters of the body, and as I will write with the help of God.

Level 4 - that the body will rule in all its details, and man will find in himself all the physical matters. But just as the soul now is in this world like a stranger in a land, and it needs to go in the ways of the body, so the body will be like a stranger in a land, and the soul is the one that rules, and the body will need to go in its ways, like the matter of (Exodus Rabbah 47:5), "When you go to a city, follow its customs." To what is this similar? To Moshe our teacher, peace be upon him, when he went to receive the Torah for Israel, behold his body was not lost and did not change, but because his body was like a guest in the place of the souls, it changed its taste to do like the deeds of the souls, and as our Sages explained (Bava Metzia 86a), "A person should never change from the custom of the place" etc., see there. It turns out, that his change at that time is not drawn because of himself but because of his place, and it is not a complete change.

Behold, there are still no consequences drawn from these matters of the body, for therefore he is still like a stranger, and as we explained, that he needs to go in the ways of the soul; but in this fourth level - all the matters of the body are discerned and known, but they are not in their place, and they need to nullify their matter because of the soul. From this level and above, not even all the details of the body are discerned, all the more so that they have no consequence, that they need to go in the ways of the soul.

Level 5 - is that the body will rule in all its aspects, and it will be like a man who rules in his house, that all his matters are in their full force and in all their consequences. Also this level is divided into two, and nevertheless it is all one level. This is because the matters of the body, even in the aspect of the body, can be in two ways, either in a secular way and the deeds of an animal, like the deeds of most people, or in a way of holiness and service, like the matter of (Proverbs 3:6), "In all your ways know Him," when everything is with proper intention as it should be and as it will be in the future in the time when it is said (Ezekiel 36:26), "And I will give you a heart of flesh," as it would have been fitting for man to be if he had not sinned. But both of them together are in any case matters of physicality, for one needs to eat, one needs to drink, and it is impossible without this, whether it is eating and drinking of secular or of holy. This and that is a physical matter.

Indeed, when we know that all these things are born from the the concealment of His face,, or from the illumination of His face, therefore we will say that the Holy One, Blessed be He, switches His guidances according to what is needed for the creature for these five levels. For at the lowest level, which is the fifth, the lowest of all, He will increase to guide with the concealment of His face, and with little illumination of His face He will guide His world; and in the fourth - He will decrease the concealment and increase the illumination; and in the third - He will decrease the concealment decrease after decrease, and the illumination will increase an additional increase; and so in this way, until ascending to the first level, that the illumination will greatly prevail, and the concealment in the slightest, until because of this no dominion will remain but for the soul alone, and not for the body at all.

Soul: Why did you need to divide this division into five levels?

Intellect: The gradation is self-evident, as all these things can exist in succession: existence without dominion; general dominion; dominion of some details; dominion of all details, yet still as a guest outside his place; and dominion of all details in their proper place, like a man ruling in his own house. These five things follow the natural order, requiring no proof or enumeration. However, what you need now is the initial division I mentioned: the complete dominion of the soul alone; some dominion of the body; and the dominion of the whole body. This is essential for understanding the entirety of the guidance. The five levels I mentioned are for your safekeeping, as I know there will be things in the words of the Sages that will require this premise to understand properly, but this is not the place for that matter.

The Three States of the World

Soul: Let us speak of these three states.

Intellect: Our Sages have taught us that the world endures for six thousand years, after which the seventh thousand is desolate, and then the Holy One, Blessed be He, renews His world. They further said about the seventh thousand, "The righteous will have wings made for them by the Holy One, Blessed be He, and they will float on the face of the water, as it is written, 'But those who hope in the Lord will renew their strength.'" From the simple meaning, we learn of three times: the six thousand years, the seventh thousand, and the renewal of the world.

During the six thousand years, the world stands as it is now. In the seventh thousand, the world is not yet renewed, and the righteous live as if in the resurrection of the dead, with wings made for them by the Holy One, Blessed be He. Finally, in the renewal of the world, the Holy One, Blessed be He, will renew the world completely. Currently, the body has complete dominion, like a man ruling in his own house. But in the seventh thousand, the righteous ascend from the earth, the body remains outside its dwelling place, like a wanderer or a lodger. Thus, it will have no dominion, just as Moshe had none when he ascended the mountain, no longer going in the way of earthly inhabitants. Our Sages called the seventh thousand "a day that is entirely Sabbath rest for eternal life," as they rest from all physical labors. Yet, the body has not departed from existence, as renewal has not yet been given to creation. However, from the renewal of the world onward, "tomorrow to receive their reward," there is no need for the body's dominion, as it is only needed for service in its time. Its existence will be secondary to the soul, to delight in the supreme good eternally.

Soul: But the seventh thousand and the renewal of the world are hidden from our knowledge. How can we speak of them?

Intellect: On the contrary, we will speak of them. We certainly know the existence and general nature of these times, which is what we are discussing regarding the body and the soul. However, we cannot comprehend the details of these times. Only the current six thousand years are known and comprehended in detail, and our discussion will revolve around this. The other two times we will know only in general, as the times when the body loses dominion and the soul ascends to its original strength.

Man's Service in This World

Soul: Then, let us speak of what we are permitted and able to comprehend.

Intellect: Now, we must understand the first state of man in this world, which is the time of his service. We have already explained the general nature of this service: to remove all deficiencies found in his creation, the evil that is present and destined to be nullified. It is man's burden to strive to nullify it first from himself and then from the entire creation as far as it pertains to him. As our Sages said, a person is obligated to say the world was created for him. Our Sages explained this matter in the Midrash on the verse, "for you have stumbled in your iniquity," with a parable of a high rock at a crossroads that people stumbled over, which the king ordered to be hewn little by little until it could be removed from the world. However, what needs explanation now are the details of this service and how this repair will be done for man and the world.

First, we must explain the existence of this evil, the cause of the entire burden of service, and know its boundaries, nature, consequences, power, how it is hewn as in the parable, and how it will pass from the world. You will see that this is a completely new existence, innovated by the Master, Blessed be He, to test human beings and give them a place for service. There was no hint or mention of this existence, nor anything close to it, before the Master innovated it, for He is the ultimate good and perfection. All that is good, even if new, relates to Him and comes close to His nature. But this evil is the very opposite of Him, having no name or mention before He innovated it. By His infinite ability, He can bring into existence even that which is opposite to Him, to make known that there is no boundary to His ability. This is what the verse says, "Who forms light etc. and creates evil, I am the Lord who makes all these." Indeed, He brought it into existence only for it to be nullified, as our Sages said, and only in the boundary, nature, and law that He desired, so that good fruit could be gathered from the evil itself for the righteous, to give them a good reward in the world.

Soul: This matter certainly needs to come to its nature, as this knowledge will include many areas.

Intellect: I need to present to you first a general and fundamental principle.

Soul: Speak.

Intellect: You need to know that all that comes into being or endures in existence does so only by an influence flowing from Him, Blessed be He, and the existence born from it is according to the existence of the influence. The Gaon Rav Moshe ben Maimon explained this well in his Guide of the Perplexed, in many chapters of part II. For example, the influence of the stars gives birth to all matters of this lower world, as our Sages said, "There is not a single herb below that does not have a mazal in the firmament that strikes it and says to it, 'Grow!' ". These influences act according to the law imprinted in them by the

Almighty, influencing only what they receive from Him. But the Almighty is the source of all flowing influence. The Gaon explained this in chapter 12, referring to the "fountain of living waters" mentioned by the prophet Jeremiah and the "fountain of life" mentioned by King David, meaning the influence of existence. When it became clear that He is incorporeal and everything is His act, we say that the world was innovated by the Creator's influence, and He influences it with all that will be innovated in it. Thus, we say that He influences of His wisdom.

You have already heard that all the acts the Master does with us are not of His simple essence, exalted above all blessing and praise, for He is exalted above all that is relevant to His creatures. Rather, they are matters He innovated by His will and desire, the kinds of influence He wanted and innovated to influence and go in the order He decreed in His wondrous wisdom, all pertaining to the existences He wanted to bring into being.

Thus, the cause and effect are both innovated from His will - the kinds of influence and their ways are the cause, and the creatures are the effect. The Master innovated kinds and ways of influence, like the kinds of existences He wanted, for each kind of influence gives birth to a single kind of existence. This is simple, as the influence of wisdom, might, and wealth are each distinct.

Soul: Is the Holy One, Blessed be He, not able to create all existences with one influence?

Intellect: Influence means what reaches from the Creator to His creatures to make some matter in them. We cannot discern it from the Actor's perspective, as we do not know how He acts. We can only discern it from the perspective of the one acted upon. When power and might reach a creature from the Creator, that influence will be the influence of might, as the Supreme Will intended it to give birth to might. When wisdom reaches, that influence will be the influence of wisdom. This is simple.

The Existence of Evil and its Role

Intellect: Let us speak of our case, the good and the bad we see being born in the world. How do you think they are influenced?

Soul: Is it not evident? What is good is an influence of beneficence, and what is bad is an influence of evil.

Intellect: I will say two things to you. First, the Holy One, Blessed be He, does not influence evil, God forbid, for He is the source of good, and no bad will come from a source of good.

Soul: If so, how does evil come? It is written, "Who makes peace and creates evil."

Intellect: It is written "creates evil," not "does evil," because He created evil in existence, for without His creation it would not exist, but He does not actively do it.

Soul: How then is it done?

Intellect: The verses state, "O Lord, by Your favor You made my mountain stand strong; You hid Your face, and I was dismayed," and "You hide Your face, they are dismayed." Moshe already said, "And I will hide my face from them and they will be devoured." This is because the good is actively done by the Holy One, Blessed be He, with His good influence, but the bad is only the absence and nullification of His influence, whether a little or a lot. For the good influence comes with all the repairs needed for the benefit of the one influenced. If the influence is completely nullified and absent, this will be a complete nullification for the one influenced. But if the influence is not completely nullified, only the conditions of its perfection are absent, there will be a deficiency in the one influenced, not a complete nullification. For example, with the influence of existence and life, when it comes complete with all good preparations, the one influenced will be alive and healthy. If it is completely nullified, the one influenced will die. But if it is not completely nullified, only its preparations and conditions of perfection are absent, the one influenced will not die but will become ill and live a life of pain. This is simple. Thus, we cannot say good and bad are two influences, as you thought, but an influence and its absence or nullification, in whole or in part.

Soul: This was the first reason. What is the second you promised to tell me?

Intellect: When we examine the existence of things, we find that evils are nothing but the corruptions of good. If we take all the kinds of existing good and evil, understanding their definitions, we will see that the existence of evils is only the corruptions of those good things. Therefore, it is inapplicable to say they are two influences, but rather an influence and its absence or nullification in whole or in part, as we have explained.

Soul: If so, this world that we see is composed of good and evil. We must say it was created in two ways, with influence and nullification of influence.

Intellect: Is this a wonder? It is simple and impossible to disagree. All that is good is born of His influence, and all that is evil is born of the absence and nullification of influence. If we see good and evil, we will certainly know that God did these two - He influenced and removed His influence, and the two creations we mentioned were created.

Soul: But I do not understand this. We can say creatures were created from influence, but how can creatures be created from the absence of influence? Existence cannot be born from absence. We must either say the Holy One, Blessed be He, actively created evil, or that it would have been impossible for it to have creation and existence.

Intellect: When we say the Holy One, Blessed be He, created this world, we understand first the creation of the general, and then the particulars - first the nature itself, and then its individuals. When the Master wanted to innovate nature in good and evil, an influence certainly came from Him to innovate the existence of nature, which is the good. And this very influence - some of it was absent, namely, the good preparations in it and the conditions of its perfection that were making nature in its good state. The existence of this absence is what innovated in nature the corruptions of the good existence, which are the entirety of evil. Nature is corrupted by the influence not being perpetuated for it.

After these two matters were innovated in the general nature, the individuals were built in particular, these according to the good matters and these according to the evil matters. The existence of the individuals is also made by influence, as we set the foundation that nothing is made except by influence. This influence is the one that comes after the influence that innovated in the general existence the creation and the corruption. Therefore, it is in its law to take from the general nature what will be needed for their composition of the good and the evil already innovated.

I am not saying the influence was completely nullified, for then all existences would have been nullified, and this absence cannot make existence. Rather, it was nullified only in part, as its preparations and repairs were nullified. This is like what reaches a man that he becomes ill and does not die. So too, the existence of the general nature is corrupted in the turning away of the influence a little, not completely, and the evils are innovated that are only corruptions in the existence of the perfect nature.

Our premise is established - the Holy One, Blessed be He, does only good, and evil He does not do, but from the absence of His influence it is born.

Soul: In conclusion, I understood the existence of evil and how it comes into being. Now we need to know all its boundaries.

Intellect: You need to know one great premise. Even though it was certainly anciently in His law to do all these deeds, as nothing changes in Him at any time, this will not be called potential things that need to become actual. This is one of the errors the believers in the eternity of the world stumbled in. The principle is that all matters of the Master before the creation of the world are incomprehensible, and none of the definitions mentioned now are applicable there. One should mention neither potentiality nor actuality, which would necessitate the existence of the relation found between them.

However, when He wanted to create the world, He Himself innovated the existence of potentiality and actuality, making the world and all creatures first in potentiality and then in actuality, to innovate this existence. In His first utterance to create the world, the world was in potentiality before going out into actuality. Our Sages hinted to this, saying, "In the beginning is also an utterance," differing from the other utterances, as here the world was included in potentiality before going out into actuality. When He innovated nature in potentiality, all these matters we mentioned were made in the influence. Afterwards, everything went out into actuality as prepared in potentiality, as we have explained.

I will inform you of a profound matter in this, the principle of the world's existence in all its times. The root is that the Master desired and wanted to influence of His goodness to the existences He wanted to bring into being. He innovated the existence of illumination and influence from Him, fitting for the level of these existences. However, what the Master desired in the influence is that it should be an influence of actual holiness from Him, the essence and source of holiness, and the consequences should be only matters of complete holiness, as it is now with the angels, who have no other matter but complete holiness. The ultimate intention in innovating this influence is none other than an influence from His holiness to His existences, to enjoy the splendor of His holiness, nothing else.

But because He wanted the existence of this lowly world, He decreed His influence should also be lowered in level to give birth to these lowly and physical things, a descent for it, as this was not the ultimate purpose for which it was innovated. What we see now, that He influences physical and lowly things, we know is a diminution and lowering for the influence itself, needing to garb itself in these inferior ways, since it is the influence of the Almighty, the source of perfection and holiness. But it arose in the thought before Him to garb His influence in these dark ways until the appointed time when it will shed all these garments and remain in its clarification and law, that the creation and all its matters should be only holy to the Lord.

During man's time of service, the influence garbs itself in these garments. When the time of service is complete, it will shed the garments. The Supreme Will placed great causes and cycles for this matter to reach its end. The root of the interchange of the world's times is the way of His influence, changing from elevation to elevation until reaching the essence of its matter, for all innovated in the existences to be only holy of holies, as we have explained.

In sum, the Master innovated an influence from Him to the existences whose ultimate matter is only drawing holiness from Him to the existences. He further innovated ways for the influence, lowly and inferior in relation to its holiness. And He innovated in the influence itself the nullifications and corruptions of order that I mentioned. All this depends on the revelation of the unity we mentioned, that from the concealment of the face all these things are innovated in the law of His influence, and from the revelation afterwards all these garments shed from it. We will speak further of this in the future with God's help.

What we need now is to know that in the influence itself the Supreme Decree innovated things, and they are the main thing found afterwards in the world, for only after all these preparations did He make this lowly world, built according to all these matters, composed of all things, to revolve from matter to matter as the Supreme Will decreed.

Soul: This premise is fundamental, to understand the many preparations required for the existence of this world, as its nature is not complete without all these preparations. Let us now complete our matter.

Intellect: We have already said that this evil that was created, was only created within the boundary that the Supreme Will desired. Even though the Master, Blessed be He, innovated nullification for existences, He only innovated it for imperfect existences. Perfect existences will have no nullification, but their endurance will be eternal. Therefore, there is now nullification for the existences of the world, but in the future there will no longer be. This is because the creation is now imperfect, so He decreed nullification upon it. But in the future, the new heavens and the new earth will be innovated with perfect creation, and thus they will have no nullification.

It turns out that the first influence, which brought into existence the general nature and the nullification of its order that brought into existence the corruptions of nature, was not an influence that would give birth to perfect things, like the new heavens and earth of the future, for they will have no nullification, as we have explained. Rather, it was an influence that did not have the law to give birth except to imperfect things, and therefore the nullification engraved for the purpose of the existence of the corruptions in nature was engraved for it.

The influence that brought into existence the individuals of nature, composed of good and evil, is an influence that separates the evils alone, so that they should not nullify the existences, but they should be limited by the power of the decree of the Place, and dependent on the utterance to not prevail and nullify the existences, but to exist in that measure and boundary needed for the nature of these existences, and to prevail at another time that needs a greater prevalence, and at another time to diminish, everything proper in its time as the Supreme Will decreed. From now on there are certainly deficiencies and corruptions in the existences, but they are not so much that they nullify them from existence, and indeed they are in a measure that ultimately they will prevail, until they nullify them, for all existence is destructible; and their existence turns out to be measured in a very precise measure, as the Supreme Wisdom knew.

You will see that the Supreme Thought that innovated the first influence that we mentioned, was intended to innovate the nullification, and therefore it did not innovate it perfect from the beginning, but only so that there should be nullification and evil in the world, as we have already explained, not out of inability and lack of power, God forbid. What is destined to be done at the end in the new earth and heavens that we mentioned, He was able to do from the beginning, but they are made imperfect so that the nullification should fall upon them. But in the second influence that He wanted to give existence to the existences, the intention of the Supreme Thought was to save the existences from the nullification, and to distance it from them until the appointed time, as we have explained, and therefore it did not nullify the nullification from the world, but limited the evils and put them in the boundary that it wanted for the purpose of the nature of the world, as we have explained, until the time will come and He will remove all the evils from existence, and all the existences will remain perfect and eternal.

Indeed you will remember now what I mentioned to you above, how the foundations of all His guidance are two attributes - the concealment of the face and the illumination of the face, whose consequences are the perfections and the deficiencies, and from this - the good and the evil. The existence of evil is not born except from the intensity of the concealment of the face, the ultimate concealment of Him; for when the Supreme Will wanted to create man with a soul and body, according to the nature that we see today in the soul and the body - He equated His attributes to grasp and act always with the two attributes, the attribute of the concealment of the face and the attribute of the illumination of the face, to be grasping this and also from that His hand should not rest, to sustain all the natures of man for good, the weak and the strong, the honorable and the lowly, all that is needed for his sustenance according to the ultimate intention in him.

However, here you need one premise, and that is, that we will not say because one creature will be lacking perfection that it is an actually evil thing, for there can be a deficiency, that even though it is not the perfection and the complete good - it is not evil. You see, the angels too are certainly lacking, for they are not in ultimate perfection, for there is no ultimate perfection but to the Master, and among them too there are several levels and grades, that the second level is inferior to the first and lacking from it, and nevertheless they are not in a deficiency so great that it should produce in them that which is actually evil, for there is no jealousy among them, no hatred, they have no evil inclination, they have no sleep and no fatigue and no illness and no death. But human beings are inferior to angels and lacking from them, and the deficiency in them prevailed so much that they have that which is evil, for they have an evil inclination, illnesses and death. Animals have in them a greater deficiency, for they have no intellect and no speech, and they are filthy and unclean.

There are the harmful ones and the angels of destruction and the spirits of impurity that are actually evil, and they are the very opposite of the good and perfection, those from whom the supreme Name is concealed with a complete concealment, like the reason, "The Holy One, Blessed be He, does not associate His Name with the evil." Indeed, it is the chain of deficiencies that brings out the evil, for in the concatenation of this matter, and deficiency added upon deficiency, ultimately it will produce that which is actually evil. Before the Master innovated the existence of the guidance that He innovated for the purpose of the existences, there was no matter for any deficiency at all, and when He innovated this existence, it turns out that the existence of one order was innovated that in its concatenation it will produce evil, for once there is existence for deficiency - its end will be actual evil.

However, one of the fundamental matters that He innovated is the matter of measure and proportion, for in His simplicity there is no applicability for any measure and any proportion, and since He wanted the law of gradation - He established everything with measure, and ordered all the existences in gradation, this under that, from the first of them to the last of them, and in each and every level He measured with His measure, how much deficiency there will be in it and how much good and repair will remain in it. According to the measured measure so are the consequences born in that level, and all their laws and all their statutes, everything as befits all, each one in its place.

It turns out that when He, may He be blessed, grasps the two attributes as one, in the concealment of the face and the illumination of the face that we mentioned, from this the soul and the body will be born, with the matters of the body being inferior to those of the soul, having the deficiencies that are not in the soul, but not because of this will there be evil in it. However, when He, may He be blessed, wanted to innovate the existence of evil, which is the very opposite of His perfection, as we have explained, then He concealed His face the greatest concealment that it is possible to think, until when He is only concealing His face and not illuminating them at all, from this will be born the creation of the very corruptions, and He created a destroyer to destroy. It turns out that the entirety of evil, which He, may He be blessed, turned back His right hand from guiding His world, and guides it with heaviness, the power of the darkness of His concealment, and placed in this nature all the corruptions of the good, they are all the attributes of the heavenly court, to bring to judgment all that is hidden and the wicked. Indeed, the wrath of the Holy One, Blessed be He, is but a moment, and He has no fury but enough for the holy and designated serpents to make Gehinnom, to strike the wicked according to his wickedness in number.

Afterwards, He returned and placed His face, as it were, to the existence of the individuals that will exist and come into being, not that they should be nullified, even though they will be susceptible to nullification. The righteous one grasped his way for repairs, not for perversions. He returned and illuminated His face upon the world destined to be created. Had He illuminated it with great illumination, the existence of the existences would have been born in ultimate repair, namely in their eternal endurance. However, He did not do so, but brought into existence existences that exist and endure, yet are not eternal. Nevertheless, He placed a way for His guidance, revolving in His circumstances all that He created for His glory to be perfected. He will illuminate His world with a great, vast, and mighty light, resulting in eternal and perfect endurance. On the contrary, this evil that He created - He will remove from the earth. Moreover, all the existences will thank Him for the good He did for them in the first days, as the prophet Isaiah informed us (Isaiah 12:1), "I will give thanks to You, O Lord, for You were angry with me," which I have already spoken of above.

Soul: Please summarize briefly what you have elaborated thus far.

Intellect: The principle is this: when the Master, blessed be He, wanted to innovate the existence of the general nature in good and evil, with its individuals composed of both, He influenced an influence that gives birth to the existence of the good in its nature, and the good was engraved in that nature. He then removed the perfection of that influence by concealing the face of His goodness completely, and all corruptions were engraved in nature. Afterwards, He influenced again with the illumination of His face to bring existences into existence - the individuals of nature composed of good and evil in one composition, existing in their current nature - existing but susceptible to corruption, not eternal. Ultimately, He will illuminate His face with a great illumination, remove the nullification from nature, and the individuals will remain perfect and eternal.

The Orders of Providence in Reward and Punishment

Intellect: Now I will explain the existence of man according to this matter of the existence of evil that we mentioned.

Soul: Speak, for I am listening.

Intellect: At first, I will put forth to you one premise, needed for its matters.

Soul: Speak.

The existence of man is built with wisdom that is deep beyond limit. The Master, blessed be He, created many great creatures, one higher than the other, all needing their watch, for there is nothing for naught. Everything stands on the fundamental cornerstone, which is what the Master, blessed be He, wants in the service of man - that he should repair all deficiencies in the creation and elevate himself elevation after elevation, until he cleaves to His holiness. He placed all matters of distance from Him and their consequences, and all matters of nearness to Him and their consequences, all of them profound and mighty, standing to revolve in great circumstances to reach the general perfection.

Indeed, the Supreme Will wanted the hand of man to reach all these matters - all moved by the movements and deeds of man. These are great mechanisms like a clock whose wheels meet each other, with a small wheel moving many large wheels. The

Master, blessed be He, tied all His creations with great ties, everything tied to man, for him to be the one who moves with his deeds, and all the rest are moved by him. He covered everything with the covering of skin and physical flesh, only this physical surface seen, but in truth, there are great mechanisms inside that the Holy One, Blessed be He, created in His world for the purpose of this entire matter for man's deeds, service, elevation, addition of holiness, or descent and inferiority, God forbid, and all his many states. This is only through the soul in all its parts and roots included in his body. King David alluded to this, saying (Psalms 40:6), "Many things you have done, O Lord my God, Your wonders and Your thoughts toward us," and (Psalms 139:14), "I will give thanks to You, for I am fearfully and wonderfully made; wonderful are Your works, and my soul knows it very well." The body does not comprehend these many things like the soul, because the thing is not seen in physicality, but in spirituality.

This is because of the depth of the great wisdom found in all the deeds of the Creator, to make everything in the best and most praiseworthy way that can be, everything in correspondence and connection of matters to matters and in proper relation. You will see, man cannot be in one time except in one place, and he needs a duration of time to move from place to place; the angels according to their honor from this body are not so, but flight was related to them for their lightness. The senses of man do not sense except in that measure and boundary engraved for them; the spiritual ones are not so at all. In sum, the very essence of the subjects and their occurrences in all their matters are always related.

It turns out that we have two discernments to discern in the matter of man and all the other creatures: 1) the existence of the matters intended in their existence and in their occurrences, meaning, the consequences born of their being and of their acts; and 2) their way, meaning, their form and the form of their acts. What will move the body will be able to move also the soul and the angel, but this one according to its way and that one according to its way. These are two attributes, great acts in His acts: 1) the fixing of what will be born of the acts of the creatures, which is the entirety of all the laws of His guidance and the orders of His mechanisms that we mentioned; and 2) the fixing how those creatures will give birth to those consequences, and also for this there are great orders that are fitting and needed for the completion of this matter. It turns out that at first, before the sin of Adam, he was on a great level, first in the main of his existence, meaning,

in the consequences of his deeds, that they reached the height of the world, as we wrote; and second in his form and in the form of his deeds in the very form of his body, for his body was already as pure as the very existence of the angels, until a fitting place for his dwelling was the Garden of Eden, which is also now a dwelling place for angels and spirits. Of this our Sages hinted (Genesis Rabbah, 20:12), in their saying, "In the Torah of Rabbi Meir they found written, garments of light." This matter has already been explained much with our Sages, that the intention in this saying is to make known the pure level of the body of Adam the first before his sin, that after the sin it thickened and became coarse and heavy as of this day. We have already seen an example of this in the world, Enoch and Elijah, that their very body was purified and elevated to be like the supreme angels. It is simple that also his movements and acts were certainly in a way that is more refined and spiritual, like the acts of Enoch and Elijah as of this day.

Soul: Why did you need to divide this division into five levels?

You will see that the Garden of Eden, which was and will be, is certainly a refined and spiritual place where spirits dwell even now. The Torah testifies that Adam was there and ate and enjoyed the fruits that grow there. Since we see that it is now a dwelling for souls, the fruits that were there must have been much more refined than the fruits of this world, like the relation of air to dust. The eating would not be appropriate for a thick and coarse body as it is today, but for a body that is refined and almost spiritual, like the bodies of Elijah and Enoch. However, according to the level of consequences born from deeds, so are the ways of those deeds, and all matters of creation correspond and equate each subject with its conditions, deeds, consequences, place, and the one who does them.
You will see that Adam's physicality before his sin was at the level of his current spirituality. Consider how his spirituality was and how far-reaching the consequences of those deeds were. It suffices to say what our Sages mentioned (Genesis Rabbah, 8:10), "The ministering angels wanted to say 'holy' before him."

We can infer what would have been fitting if he had not sinned and ascended to the great elevation designated for him. Just as we see that his physicality then is like the spirituality of now, we can deduce that his physicality, if he had ascended, could have been like the level of spirituality then, for things ascend from elevation to elevation.

Indeed, this is the matter of the two trees - the tree of life and the tree of knowledge. Certainly, a verse does not depart from its plain meaning; the trees were trees, the fruits were fruits, and the eating was eating, but refined fruits and refined eating beyond our imagination, which only perceives physical things. Even in physical fruits, there are properties used for medicines and other wondrous things in their natural properties. These trees had properties engraved by the Creator in their fruit. The tree of life had a property to bring proper knowledge, cleaving, and love to Him, and to negate physical lusts from the soul. The tree of knowledge had the opposite effect, bringing physical lusts, materiality, and all sins.

If Adam had eaten from the tree of life and not from the tree of knowledge, he would have cleaved to and delighted in the holiness of his Maker for all eternity without separation. When he ate from the tree of knowledge, he sank into physical lusts and loved materiality. Since this was so, measure for measure, he lost the preciousness of his spirituality and remained physical for the decreed number of days until he would be satiated with the fruit of his sin and return healed. The great principle (Makkot 23a), "Once he was lashed, he is like your brother," then he will return to his original strength, and his existence will be completed.

This is the first part of evil, and the second is the corruptions and ruin, as we have explained. Corruptions do not fall except in this lowly physical form, and in every superior form, they do not fall. In Adam himself, in his more repaired and superior form, there was no illness or harm falling upon him. All this was certainly prepared from the beginning, and in the creation of evil itself, all these were made in the law of general nature, even though you have heard of the prior lowering in man from the time of his creation.

It turns out that the Master, blessed be He, first innovated the influence needed for man's perfect and superior existence, which is a supreme existence in potentiality for man. Afterwards, He wanted to lower his existence, so there would remain a place for him to perfect himself in his ascent to that supreme level befitting him. The influence is what is first lowered, its power weakens, and its level and law are lowered, so that it no longer gives birth to man in this elevation, but in his lowering and deficiency. The main thing is that this influence should be prevented from giving birth to its consequence in elevation and perfection, not because there will only be a small and little power in its law, for this would not have been called a lowering, but that the prevention should be outside of it. Even though from its law it would have been fitting for the perfect consequence to be born from it, this thing will be absent from it because of the innovated evil, which causes it this lowering.

This is the matter like the verses (Deuteronomy, 32:18), "The Rock that bore you, you neglected," (Numbers, 14:16), "because the Lord was not able," which are expounded by our Sages (see Berachot 32a), as it were, His power weakened like a female. With the lowering of the influence in the weakness of its power, a place is found for actual evil.

I will now come to a matter that I mentioned at the beginning, that the Master, blessed be He, did not engrave nullification and corruption for perfect creatures, but for imperfect creatures. Therefore, when the creatures will be perfected in the future, there will no longer be any nullification for them at all. What I need to explain now is what this deficiency of perfection is that gives birth to the nullification. You will see here profound wisdom in the matter of His guidance and the great preciousness of Israel.

Soul: I desire nothing more than to know these things completely in their essence, each thing and its consequences. Therefore, I will greatly rejoice in this knowledge that you will impart to me.

The intellect said - Whoever looks at the parts of this creation according to what their eyes see will at first only perceive them as scattered and separate matters, not all connected to one purpose, but each one a matter on its own for a specific purpose, complete in itself without needing its fellow. There are many species in the inanimate, plants, and animals, with no apparent connection or relation between them that they need to help each other and gather for one purpose. Each one was created for what it was created, and its matters are complete for the intended purpose, no more. Nevertheless, an orderly gradation is certainly seen in all of nature. Whoever contemplates the existence of the existents will find them all in gradation, beginning from the heavens above, descending to the earth below, and contemplating all the species, they will find them all one under the other in an orderly, proper gradation.

But one who delves into wisdom will find that all existents are completely connected to each other, all needed to complete the matter to which the supreme wisdom intended in the creation. They all gather for one purpose, whose conditions are many and order is very deep. These are all the many parts of creation. Therefore, they all relate to each other in the order that the supreme thought wanted. From all of them will emerge the good fruit worthy to emerge from the creation. This matter is very deep, for here wisdom expands and goes to infinity, to know the purpose of all existents and what reached them in this general intention.

Our Sages said (Avot end of ch. 6), "Everything that the Holy One, Blessed be He, created in His world - He did not create it except for His glory." Indeed, one needs to understand this matter of glory, for it too is an innovation with Him, like all the other descriptions, as explained above. When we understand this description, we will understand the purpose of all these creatures in completing this glory, how they are all needed for its completion, and how they all gather to this purpose. For now, it suffices for us to know only in one general principle - that all matters of creation are connected and gather to the one purpose. We shall know, therefore, that their matter is not complete in that they exist each one to its end, but in that they are connected to each other and unite for the one purpose; for this alone is the completeness of their matter, since this is what is more necessary for the purpose for which they were created, which is the general purpose.

In truth, you will see that also in actions, there is no evil that exists in the world except in the parts of things before they combine to complete the thing, but there is no complete thing that will be evil. Since we know that everything the Holy One, Blessed be He, does is only very good, that which appears lacking on one side in one of the conditions of things is completed by another condition. That lack was only because that thing was not completed in all its conditions; when it is completed, it is certainly good.

This matter is verified from the action itself, the general action which is the revolution of the world. The matter will become clear that it too is so at the end of everything, at the time when the promise will be fulfilled (Isaiah 12:1), "I will thank You, O L-rd, for You were angry with me," for then all the parts of the act will be completed, and the act will be only truly good. Therefore, it is said that at first the Master, blessed be He, prepared nature as we explained, each species in it according to the existence of the species, each one by itself in the gradation of their existence. In this matter, there was negation and destruction, which is the destruction found in each species according to its existence. But the matter of their connection and gathering to the general purpose is a correction for this matter, for with this they emerge from under the hands of evil and are saved from it.

This is the matter that we already mentioned, that everything the Holy One, Blessed be He, created in His world, He created only for His glory. The glory is that He will rejoice in all His works and have a place, as it were, to delight all His works with His goodness. The conduct in all the works is only to bring everything to the complete correction, so that there will no longer be any existence of evil at all. But this fruit emerges only in the gathering of all the works together. It is found that in the species of nature by themselves, not in terms of their connection, the negation and all the lowliness and destruction occurred, but in their connection, their correction and salvation from the evils is rooted.

Soul: These are clear matters that settle the heart. But you still need to explain the matter of the preciousness of Israel that you promised to explain, for I do not yet see its relevance here.

Intellect: I explained the different matters in the influence that cause the difference of the products which are the events that are born in the world; however, the first cause for all this, the reason for the difference of the matters in the influence, is the matter that depends on Israel which I mentioned to you. Now I will explain. The Holy One, Blessed be He, is with Israel like a father to his son, like a man to his wife of his youth, that all His desire is to us, as stated (Song of Songs 7:11), "I am my beloved's, and his desire is toward me." It is written (Psalms 40:6), "Many things You have done, O L-rd my G-d; Your wonders and Your thoughts are toward us," and (Leviticus 26:9), "And I will turn to you" etc. "and multiply you." The Holy One, Blessed be He, desires, as it were, to delight in His creatures and rejoice in them, as stated (Psalms 104:31), "The L-rd shall rejoice in His works."

In His truly turning to them, out of His love for them, from the joy that He rejoices in them, as it were, He thinks thoughts, does not cease to do good to them and to multiply them, constantly renews His goodness to them, influence after influence, in every way most suitable for their correction and benefit, as the father who turns with his love to his son would think. The main thing in all this is Israel, for His desire is to them, like the words of the verse, "I am my beloved's, and his desire is toward me." All the rest of creation depends only on them, for when He turns to them with love, He will only constantly renew goodnesses after goodnesses for the whole world, true and complete goodnesses.

However, the sin is severe, to cause the Holy One, Blessed be He, to turn away from Israel, like a husband who is angry with his wife or a father with his son. About that time it is said (Genesis 6:6), "And G-d regretted that He had made them," for He is not happy about the world and His creatures, then all influence is absent, and success departs. It is found that the creation of evil is not born except from the concealment of the face, that the Master, blessed be He, did not turn with love to the lower ones and did not rejoice in them. This is a cause for all the absence of the influence that we mentioned.

You will see that the Holy One, Blessed be He, foresaw the deeds of the righteous and the deeds of the wicked. Our Sages taught us this in the Midrash, where they said (Bereishit Rabbah 2:5), "From the beginning of the creation of the world, the Holy One, Blessed be He, foresaw the deeds of the righteous and the deeds of the wicked," and (Bereishit Rabbah 8:4), "What did the Holy One, Blessed be He, do - He removed the way of the wicked from before His face, and partnered His mercy in it and created it."

That is, all the creation of the world from the beginning was in the way of foreseeing the future, for He would foresee what was destined to be and establish orders for the need of all the future. In the foresight of the deeds of the righteous, there was joy for Him, and from this was born all the order of the good influence. In the foresight of the deeds of the wicked, there was all the absence of influence and damage. From then on, the law of conduct remained in this way, for the deeds of the righteous will give birth to joy for Him, which is the source of all good things, while the deeds of the wicked will sadden the heart, which is the source of all evils.
You will see that if the Master, blessed be He, had not foreseen the deeds of the wicked, the world would have had no existence at all. But He left the deeds of the wicked, for they are not

forever, but on the contrary, they cease and are nullified. He grasped the deeds of the righteous, for they are the ones that stand to exist forever and ever, and with their power He created and sustained His world. He also engraved in it for the good to grow and go, until the evil passes and is completely nullified from the world.

It is found in truth that all the orders of the supreme conduct and all its products are based only on Israel, in the turning of His goodness to them with love or in turning away from them. They alone are found to be the main thing in all of creation, and all the rest depend on them. I will not elaborate on this now. What we need for our matter is what I mentioned at first, that in His turning with love to the lower ones, all the corrections of the influence depend, and the opposite in His turning away from them.

Up to here we have completed all that is necessary to know regarding the creation of evil. Now let us explain what the Master, blessed be He, has arranged for its correction and to remove it from creation, so that all existents will be corrected to the end of the complete correction that will be in the future to come.

Indeed, what one needs to know first is that although the Supreme Will has innovated imperfections, as we have already explained, the intention was not to leave them, but on the contrary, to remove them and bring about complete rectification afterwards. Therefore, He decreed that the imperfection should not be a complete nullification that would leave no trace of what is nullified, but rather made them imperfections that can be rectified, so that the existence of created beings would continue even amidst the imperfections, until it would return to its original state, like a patient who is healed.

You can see the truth of this matter in all worldly affairs, for the imperfections were not placed to destroy the good, but to distort it, and afterwards they will be removed and the good will return to its original state. Look, even death, which is the greatest nullification in the world, is not a complete nullification, for there is the resurrection of the dead, that although the body returns to dust, the luz bone within it is preserved as is known (see Vayikra Rabbah 18:1), to rebuild from it that very same body. All the more so that which is less than death is certainly not a complete nullification, but becomes impaired and can be rectified.

Israel in exile has been brought down to the dust, as it is said of them (Lamentations 3:6), "He has made me dwell in darkness like those long dead." Yet it is written (Leviticus 26:44), "Yet for all that, when they are in the land of their enemies, I will not reject them, nor will I abhor them so as to destroy them" etc., and (Malachi 3:6), "For I, the Lord, do not change; therefore you, O children of Jacob, are not consumed." That is, the Holy One, Blessed be He, does not regret His good deeds so as to despise them. Although He allows them to become impaired, He does not abandon or forsake them completely, but allows them to suffer, knowing that it will ultimately be for their good. Therefore, He sustains their existence, but allows them to be refined in the crucible of trials of many severe troubles.

Afterwards, they will return and blossom like a vine, sprout anew like the earth brings forth its growth, as a garden causes its plantings to spring forth. The seeds themselves are proof of this, for they decay beneath the earth, but are not nullified, but rather will return from the dust and sprout. Thus, we find that the Blessed Master did not create complete nullification that has no rectification for His works, but an impairment that can be rectified.

As we have explained, for the existence of this nullification, the Blessed Master did not designate His Name of perfection upon it, for He does not designate His Name upon evil. On the contrary, it is of His perfect deeds to sustain every good thing, even within the corruptions at the time of their impairment. He does not cease hovering over them to sustain the good, so that it not be completely nullified.

You can see this matter clearly explained regarding man, as we explained above the parallel between human affairs and the affairs of the supreme providence. When a man dies, his soul leaves him, and the dust returns to the earth as it was. The hint and the matter are one, for man is built of the darkness of corporeality, which is the dark, innovated body in the concealment of His blessed countenance, as we have explained, and of the spirituality that enlivens him and refines him, born of the illumination of His blessed countenance to complete the deficiency of His creations, as we have also explained. When the Blessed Master conducts Himself with man in this order, man also lives in his world.

But when the Blessed Master ceases to shine His countenance upon him and leaves the darkness that is in his nature alone, then the soul departs from that body, and the body remains dead like a silent stone. It will even decay and be destroyed, for the Blessed Master has removed His countenance from it. It is written (Psalms 104:29), "You hide Your face, they are dismayed; You take away their spirit, they expire and return to their dust."

However, since the Blessed Master does not completely hide the face of His goodness from the world forever, for some spark of His light illuminates the darkness of the concealment of the countenance for the sustenance of the world, therefore this body is also not completely nullified, and the soul does not completely abandon it. Rather, what our holy Sages received is fulfilled - the presence with the bones in the grave of some part of life called in their language "the breath of the bones," which sustains the dead for the purpose of resurrection, so that those who arise in the resurrection will not be new creations, but those very ones who already died. Scripture states (Isaiah 58:11), "And satisfy your soul in drought, make your bones flourish."

Soul: All these things are certainly agreeable to the heart, for the Blessed Master will not despise the labor of His hands, but will sustain the good and remove the evil from it through the cycles of its circumstances.

Order of the rectification of the world

Intellect: Now we will begin with the order of the rectification of the world. We will say that you have already heard that at the time when the blessed Creator first innovated the influence for the purpose of this nature, when He was still destined to innovate the nullification for that influence, the true intention in innovating the influence was not for it to be sustained, but rather to be nullified, as we have already explained above. However, when He wanted to innovate the existence of a rectified influence to be sustained and give birth to the necessary products in the world, the intention was indeed to distance from it the evil that had already been innovated for its matter. Here the intention is the exact opposite of the first intention, as we have explained. This is the head and first of the existence of the rectification of creation - for the intention to be reversed to doing good and sustaining it, saving it from evil.

The Blessed Master has prepared all the attributes of His influence and its levels, level by level in its rectification, so that the intention in it will be only to give birth to good. He distanced from it the evil, which is the nullification, whose existence had already been innovated to befall the matter of that level. In this way He prepared all the levels of His influence in their gradation. For each of them, He needed to do all this, meaning, first - to reverse the intention in it only to the rectification of the good for the birth of existence as we have explained; second - to distance from it the nullification that had already been innovated for it so that it would not return and nullify it.

However, He also did not want to nullify the evil, but to distance it, yet for it to be existing and standing for as long as necessary for the creations. The sustenance of the evil itself will also only be from His blessed power, for He alone certainly does good and evil, but this is only the lowest matter related to His influence and providence.

We find that the Blessed Master has certainly arranged all the gradation of His influences for what is needed for the sustenance of the world, level after level, and after all these, He also related to Him the doing of evil and all its parts and matters. There is in this evil that which corresponds to all the parts of the good influence, for every part of good influence - so was nullification innovated, and from every part of good influence the nullification designated for it was distanced, but not nullified. However, all the nullifications designated for all the parts of good influence are only types of one genus, which is the general evil, and the entire genus as a whole is only related to His blessed influence in the lowest respect of all the matters included in this.

Therefore, from the time the supreme level of influence was rectified, for example, its nullification was already known and distanced from it; it was not nullified, but its existence depends on being sustained and conducted only at the lowest level designated for influence. At the second level that was rectified, its nullification was also already known, and its existence depends until the lowest level as we explained, but in terms of the gradation of influences, its matter has already come closer to coming into being than it was at first, and more so at the third than the second, and so on, until the last level.

Therefore, we say that as soon as the Blessed Master wants to completely rectify the influence, He takes to arranging the orders of good and the orders of evil. The orders of good proceed and are rectified in their levels, but the evil is suspended and standing from the beginning of the arrangement of the influence until it reaches the last level, on which all the arrangements of its matters depend in their details, for the intention is to lower the existence of evil, so that its matter will only be the least of all matters in creation. This lowering is of the great rectifications for the world, that the measure of good will be much greater than the measure of punishment.

Therefore, from the beginning of the arrangement of the orders, the Blessed Master separated the orders of good to one side to be arranged and rectified, and the orders of evil to be cycled in their lowering from level to level. For according to what order of the orders of good was rectified, so was the order of evil lowered correspondingly, until with the completion of the orders of good to be rectified, evil is found to be completely lowered, and the world is properly rectified. This is a great opening to understand the matter of "I will fill the ruins" (Ezekiel 26:2), mentioned by our Sages (Megillah 6a), for this is the entire matter of man's service, for God made good and evil, and the lowering of evil depends only on the strengthening of good, and the opposite to the opposite, God forbid. The Holy One, blessed be He, has made known to us the actions required to strengthen the good in its orders, from which the lowering of evil and all its orders naturally follows, and the world is found to be rectified with complete rectification.

Soul: All these things are clear to me. This is a proper order to understand the attributes of the Blessed Master, which are founded in the depth of His wisdom, so that the affairs of the world and its events should not be things that happen by chance. Rather, everything is arranged with profound wisdom for a perfect purpose.

Intellect: Let us complete the order of arranging His blessed judgments. We will say that behold, after the Supreme Will has already set the boundary of evil and engraved its matters that they should be and not increase, He returned and established a just conduct as the world needs after the existence of this evil in His creation. Indeed, the entirety of what the Supreme Will wanted with the existence of this evil is that it should continue for some time as He has set for it, and that afterwards it should be nullified. From the beginning of the world He is already leading it towards its good end - that the evil will be nullified from it. This is indeed one conduct that we mentioned above regarding the revelation of His unity. However, for all the time that He wants it to continue, a different conduct is needed, for its existence is not in vain, but for the purpose of man's service. Therefore, a conduct is needed here that is appropriate for the performance of this service in all its conditions.
You should certainly know that good deeds are of no benefit to Him at all, and evil deeds are of no detriment. It has already been said (Job 35:6-7), "If you have sinned, what do you

accomplish against Him," etc., "if you are righteous, what do you give Him," etc. Rather, He has created one type of conduct with special laws and ways, which He knew to be proper for this purpose, that through them there would be the existence of merit and liability for man, that according to these ways man's benefit could be called what people fulfill of the commandments, and detriment - that they transgress them; not benefit and detriment to Himself, but to what He wants to effect in us.

This is the matter of "when Israel does the will of the Omnipresent they add strength to the might above" etc., as our Sages explained (Yalkut Shimoni, Ha'azinu, end of §945). Moreover, not because He is unable to act except according to the actions of those below, God forbid, but because He does not want to act. Therefore, good deeds are called His honor, and evil deeds the opposite. Thus, this is what the Blessed Master first innovated in this conduct for the purpose of service, namely the existence of the benefit that good deeds can bring, and the detriment that evil deeds can bring, for all this is innovated and depends only on His blessed will, as we have explained. This is called the conduct of good and evil, for the entirety of good is all the rectified orders and all the benefit that results from good deeds; evil is the opposite of this - all the detriment that results from transgressions.

After this is needed to arrange matters of reward and punishment, levels of man according to his deeds, and ways of rectification through repentance and suffering.

After this, it is necessary to arrange the matters of reward and punishment, meaning what good will be given to those who fulfill the commandment, and the punishment for those who transgress it. This reward and punishment needs to be of two types, meaning reward and punishment of this world, and the true recompense of the World to Come. It is necessary to innovate the arrangements of the state of people, the state of the good and the state of the wicked, in their proximity and distance from Him in a precise gradation according to the matter of their deeds; the rectification of the corrupted, which is the general matter of repentance, or acceptance of suffering in this world or in the World to Come. This entire conduct is needed for all the time of the existence of evil. You can already see how much profound wisdom is needed to properly establish all these things.

All this is besides the profound conduct that encompasses all of existence as a whole to complete rectification, cycling things so that evil will be completely nullified from creation, and what is needed for it in terms of conduct. This is a conduct based on the concealment of the supreme perfection, and on its return to be revealed. The measure of this conduct is the measures of the cycle of this sphere, meaning the process of the entire matter that revolves and proceeds from the concealment of the supreme perfection until its revelation, as we have explained in its place with the help of Heaven. These are two conducts that we need to explain very well, if not their details, for they have no end, but at least their generalities, to the extent that our reach allows.

Soul: These are two very, very great roots, and it is certainly necessary for much wisdom and profound knowledge to be included in them.

Reward and Punishment

Intellect: Now we will first explain the conduct of reward and punishment, which is more.

Soul: Speak, for I am listening.

Intellect: First, I will tell you in general - two that are three first principles of this conduct, and afterwards we will come to their details one by one, so that the path will be paved before you. Behold, with the Holy One, blessed be He, effecting in us the effects that He effects in the designated orders and ways that He wanted, it is necessary that we distinguish two types of laws that He has decreed in this matter. The first type - all that depends on His blessed actions, which is the entirety of the ways and laws of His influence; the second - all that depends on our being affected in our reception from Him, which is the entirety of the ways and laws of our reception from Him.

Indeed, the first law, which is the law of His influence, is also divided into two; for Scripture calls (Deuteronomy 8:5), "As a man chastens his son, so the Lord your God chastens you," meaning that the chastisement with which the Holy One, blessed be He, chastens Israel is not a chastisement of vengeance and the blow of an enemy, but out of love that He loves them like a father loves his son, as it is written (Proverbs 13:24), "He who spares his rod hates his son, but he who loves him disciplines him early." Thus, the chastisement is born of love itself, and open rebuke is found to be born of hidden love. Two good consequences emerge from this root: 1 - that the chastisement itself, even at the time it is done, is not done with cruel wrath, but with great sweetening, because of the hidden love that does not allow anger to rule and be cruel; the second - that since even when the Blessed Master brings His creatures to judgment, His hidden intention is only to have mercy and to do good, sometimes if He sees that those being judged do not have the strength to bear the judgment - He turns to them with mercy and ceases His hand from judgment completely, which is the matter of (Avodah Zarah 3b), "He rises from the throne of judgment and sits on the throne of mercy." We now have to understand all these three with a clarification of their details, and the conditions that complete their matter.

Indeed, I must first present to you an introduction that is necessary for all that we will explain afterward. It is a very clear introduction for those who are accustomed to wisdom and its proofs.

Soul: Speak.

Intellect: The great rabbi Maimonides was awakened to the description of "birth" found in the Scriptures, which is applied to things in which birth is not specific. He said (Guide for the Perplexed, Part I, Chapter 7), "Birth - this word is borrowed for the existence of natural things - 'Before the mountains were born' (Psalms 90:2). It is also borrowed for the innovations of thoughts, what it necessitates of the opinions and agreements, as (Psalms 7:15), 'And gives birth to falsehood,' and from it, it is said (Isaiah 2:6), 'And they please themselves in the children of strangers.'" This description has been copied to thought and all that resemble it. Just as we borrow the description of birth for something new, so too we borrow pregnancy for something that has the potential to be actualized, as the verse itself says (Psalms 7:15), "He who is pregnant with trouble and gives birth to falsehood." For one to whom one action is copied, all its other details will also be copied. We know that every agreement of counsel that is decreed with sound reason has its parents, which are the first premises. The offspring is in its parent in potential before it is born from it, and when it is born - it goes from potential to actual.

Moreover, since everything that is perfected, its perfection is something added to its existence, for it is possible for it to exist without that perfection. However, two things reach the cause of that thing, namely its existence and its perfection, for the creative cause is the perfecting and sustaining cause, for the perfection of the effect is only the perfection of the birth of the cause, for when it gives birth to all that it has the power to give birth to, that which is born will be found complete with all its perfection. All this is simple for one who has walked the paths of wisdom.

You have heard above that all matters of existence are interconnected with each other, until they are all drawn one after the other and born from each other. All of them together are one connection, one general existence, which is not complete except with all these details. On this depends the beauty and perfection of the world, as we have explained above. This gives us a very wide space to contemplate and delve into the wisdom of the Creator in His creation. For every matter that is found in His conduct - we know that it has in the conduct itself a previous matter that necessitates it, and it is called its cause and parent. This cause is what gives birth, and it is what perfects the matter that is necessitated and born from it. This is the general principle of the preparations that we mentioned above, which revolve in the world from the highest heavens to the depths of the earth, with all the upper and lower, high and low existences being connected to each other and born and necessitated from each other. When the Master, blessed be He, bestows one of His bestowals, we do not discern in it only what it will do in the world, but also what is included in its law to further beget a matter that is necessitated by it. What follows from it in existence will always be with a view to that matter that is included in its law.

If the Master, blessed be He, further wishes and brings out from potential to actual that necessitated matter, then also in the world He will bring about a matter that is more notable and distinguished, which will be drawn from what was renewed in the bestowal in actuality; which at first was only viewed in general in what was affected by the first bestowal, now its existence is renewed in actuality. Also in this, its existence will be tested in imperfection and perfection. All these are simple matters for those who know the ways of the demonstrative sciences. When we stand to contemplate His creations in these ways and judgments, we will find great and deep wisdom, and many secrets of the Torah will be understood by us. Many doubts and difficulties found in the matter of governance and faith will be resolved for one who does not know these ways.

Soul: There is no doubt in my mind that it is impossible to grasp even that small amount that man can grasp in the wisdom of His deeds, except through the ways of learning and wisdom. Whoever wants to enter into these inquiries without the preparations and studies necessary for him - is nothing but arrogance, and he will not be able to succeed.

Intellect: Let us now speak about what we are engaged in, which is the attribute of His upright and established judgment. This is because the existence of this world at this time, which is the entire time of man's service in all its matters and its products, depends only on the attribute of His judgment, because this is the world and time that the Master, blessed be He, has prepared to show in it the uprightness of His judgment. The matter of this world is not established except by the doing of this judgment in its uprightness, as it is written (Psalms 9:17), "The Lord is known by the judgment He executes," it is written (Isaiah 5:16), "But the Lord of hosts is exalted in justice," and it is written (Proverbs 29:4), "The king by justice establishes the land." That is, it is not good for the world at all that the Holy One, blessed be He, allows the wicked to run wild and raise their heads, and the righteous are oppressed and the accuser prevails. This is certainly not good for the world, but bad.

But the good is, on the contrary, that the Holy One, blessed be He, executes judgment, subdues the wicked and lowers the haughty, exalts the righteous and lifts up their honor, as it is said (Proverbs 21:15), "When justice is done, it brings joy to the righteous," and "When the wicked perish, there are shouts of joy" (Proverbs 11:10).

It turns out that the time when the Holy One, blessed be He, gives the wicked a long rope, that they prevail in the world and destroy uprightness and righteousness, this is not called for Him, as it were - sleep. When He awakens from this sleep, it is said of Him (Psalms 78:65-66), "Then the Lord awoke as from sleep, etc. He beat back His enemies." This is because if the Holy One, blessed be He, really wanted to direct His world only with kindness and complete beneficence, so that there would be no evil in the world but only good - this would be called an establishment for the world; but it would be necessary that there be no existence of sins at all, that deeds that impair the good and distort it not be done, as will be in the future to come, as it is written (Psalms 104:35), "Let sinners be consumed from the earth," as our Sages said (Berachot 10a), "Sinners is written."

Then it would be said that the world is directed only with kindness, that is, there would be no evil inclination, but people would serve God by compulsion, as it is written (Ezekiel 36:27), "And I will cause you to walk in My statutes." But for the Holy One, blessed be He, to wait for the wicked until their measure is full, so that in any case the world will be nothing but chaos and void, and in the end the wicked will perish - this is certainly not kindness, but a very harsh judgment. For on the contrary, we have already mentioned above the saying of the verse (Proverbs 3:24), "And he who loves him disciplines him early"; it is written (Amos 3:2), "You only have I known of all the families of the earth; therefore I will punish you for all your iniquities," as our Sages said (Avodah Zarah 4a) that the Holy One, Blessed be He, exacts punishment from Israel little by little, so that evil will not increase upon them, that they will need to be diminished, God forbid, but on the contrary, He wants their correction, as we have explained.

It turns out that when the Holy One, blessed be He, desires His world, He sits, as it were, to constantly direct it with judgment, to cleanse it of all evil that is born in it little by little, then the matters of the world are found to be corrected and blessed, and they all succeed with great success. But if, God forbid, there is no merit in the world, and wickedness prevails greatly, then the Holy One, blessed be He, says (Deuteronomy 32:20), "I will hide My face from them," and it is written (Deuteronomy 31:18), "I will surely hide My face on that day." Immediately darkness prevails, wickedness and foolishness, wisdom is lowered, truth is cast down, and all matters of the world are corrupted and destroyed. Our Sages have already said (Sotah 49a), there is no day that does not have its curse, etc., even the taste of the fruits is taken away (ibid. 48a), there is no success, not in physical matters and not in spiritual matters.

If indeed the intention of the Holy One, blessed be He, was only to punish the wicked, the world would have already been destroyed because of them. But since His intention is only to do good, His discipline and rebuke are only out of love, as we have explained, therefore He wanted to establish the existence of the world even at a time when there is no merit, that this existence will not change and will not totter. He will use for this purpose His exaltedness and dominion, for He is not subjugated to any law, and He has no coercion, therefore He can sustain the world even if people are not proper. However, you must understand this matter well, for there are many distinctions in it, for it would seem that a sinner is rewarded, that the world will endure without needing merit, and will endure with the attribute of kindness and love under the sins of the wicked.

But when you discern all that needs to be discerned in this matter, you will find deep wisdom in the orders of His conduct. This is because you have already heard that the Master, blessed be He, innovated only by His will even the existence of the deficiency caused by sins, and the existence of the benefit caused by good deeds; He arranged orders of conduct that are established and upright, revolving around this axis, and on these depend the success of this world in all its matters. In His holding fast to His judgment according to all these orders, the world will succeed in all its parts. If sins cause that the Holy One, blessed be He, will be, as it were, abhorrent of the people of the world, and distance Himself from them, then these orders of conduct will be confused, for the Master, blessed be He, will not hold fast to them, and the corruptions will be found in all matters of the world, God forbid. But if He holds fast to them to establish them properly - all creatures will come to their place in peace.

There is another conduct, another time, which is when merit increases in Israel, as we explained above, at the time when the world is completely corrected, which is that the Holy One, blessed be He, will change the state of the world for the better, and will abolish from it all evil, that is, there will be no evil inclination in the souls, and no harm and loss in any creature, then the world will be conducted with great correction. This will be a correction for the world, because the world will be ready and prepared for this conduct, for evil will be abolished from it, and then judgment will no longer be needed, but it will be conducted with complete mercy and perfect beneficence. All that is now hidden from the inhabitants of the earth, because the place causes them to be so, it being a place where darkness prevails for the purpose of service, that is, for the trial of man as we have explained, will be revealed in the future to come, as it is said (Isaiah 40:5), "And the glory of the Lord shall be revealed," etc.

However, there is a time when the Holy One, blessed be He, distances Himself, as it were, from His world. His judgment is not executed, His dominion is not revealed, and it would be fitting for the world to be destroyed. But even at that time, the Holy One, blessed be He, wants the world to endure. He sustains it only with the power of His dominion, for from the perspective of judgment, it is not fit to endure. He uses His exaltedness, which is not impaired and not lacking due to the sins of people, to sustain the world so that it will not perish. But He does not increase goodness and affluence for it. On the contrary, He gives it only a constricted existence, only what is impossible without it, in order that it may endure. For the world is not corrected to be conducted with this beneficence. Not only does evil not depart from it, but it prevails in it even more. But the Holy One, blessed be He, wants His works not to perish. By the power of His unique dominion, He sustains it, even if justice dictates that it should be destroyed, but only with great constriction, as we have explained.

Then it is known that the world is fit to be conducted according to the way of His judgment. Its correction depends on this, and this is indicated by the constriction that we mentioned and the evil that prevails. Nature does not rise to goodness as it will in the future to come. On the contrary, it stands in the laws that the Master, blessed be He, has decreed for it according to the order of the judgmental conduct. But because the Holy One, blessed be He, has distanced and hidden Himself from the world, the judgment is not executed. The earth was chaos and void, and the wicked rule the world with brazen faces, like an evil beast in the forest. There is none who seeks or searches, and everything is distorted and corrupted. Only the Holy One, blessed be He, sustains His world with the power of His will that is not subjugated to any law, mere sustenance until His judgment comes to light, as it is written, "And I will make My justice rest as a light of the peoples." When we examine all the different states in the world in the matter of the revelation of His judgment or its concealment, we find them in a gradation arranged in a great order. They are five, as we will explain. You will see them one by one in their times, which were and will be until the end of the world's perfection that will be in the future to come.

The first time was the entire two thousand years of chaos, especially in the exile of Egypt. This is a time when God completely hides from His world, as if the Lord has forsaken the earth. He does not see or hear the deeds of men. The attribute of judgment does not operate in the world at all, but it is necessary for the existence of the world, obligated by the order that God has arranged. In His love for His creatures, He contemplates what to do for them to bring them to complete correction. However, He only thinks but does not act, for He hides His established judgment, leaving the world in chaos and void.

When the Holy One, blessed be He, hides His judgment, the world goes into corruption, chaos, and void. The conduct will either be with kindness or with judgment. If the conduct is with kindness, it will be good for all; if the conduct is with judgment, then the corruptions found in the world are products of the attribute of His justice and the concealment of His goodness. This concealment is done because sins cause the Holy One, blessed be He, to hide His face from His world, which is certainly judgment.

The root of all the existence of good and evil in this world is because God has hidden the face of His goodness and taken this attribute that gives place to evils from the aspect of the concealment of His face, as it is said, "He made darkness His hiding place." There are two ways in this attribute. The first is in giving place for evils to prevail and rule without His judgment rising against them to cleanse the world. The second way also depends on the concealment of His face, but it is good for the world and its creatures. His orders of conduct will be arranged in upright judgment, by the power of which the world will be cleansed of evils, not in the way of kindness that wipes away transgressions, but in the way of judgment that winnows all evil through punishments. Until the future time arrives when God will wipe out sins, there is no way for the world to be cleansed except through the uprightness of judgment.

In truth, God does not despise the labor of His hands forever and does not forsake or abandon the world. Rather, at a time when it appears as if the world is abandoned by Him, He is innovating goodness for His world, and His thoughts are always only for its rectification, not for its corruption. He conceals His counsel with great concealment, and then the world is found to be as if abandoned, with people suffering the punishments of their sins. This builds a general principle that for every elevation that God wants to give to a person or to the world, the entire time the good is destined, it comes through the depth of a hidden counsel, and therefore distress will precede it.

The first level in the states of this world is when His blessed judgment is concealed and not revealed to cleanse the evils from the earth. At that time, the Blessed One is not known in

His world. We have already said when this time was, namely, at the time of the Egyptian exile.

The second state is a time like this time, when there is no prophet or seer, and we do not have signs or wonders to compel all people to recognize His greatness. However, there will be some greater revelation and some knowledge of His greatness. The Egyptian exile was certainly not like the exile before it or after it, for Israel was immersed in labor, there was no Torah, and Israel was not a nation distinguished in its laws and commandments as it is today. People did not recognize the name of the Blessed Master at all. However, now there is Torah, and even though we are in exile, it is not called a time of chaos, as they called the first two thousand years, for there is the Torah, and the name of the Blessed Master is known among the nations.

The third state is a time when the Holy One, blessed be He, seizes dominion over His world with signs and wonders, revealed to all the nations, to know that the Lord God is in Israel, namely, all the time of the First and Second Temples. Indeed, even this revelation is an external revelation, meaning that there is no revelation here except in terms of actions alone by virtue of the visible wonders, and if those wonders were lacking, the faith would not be clarified. However, this is not the ultimate revelation that God wants His glory to be revealed in His world.

The fourth state is that God will be revealed to all His creatures in terms of knowledge and comprehension, not in terms of wonders, but that they will see His blessed glory and comprehend Him with an abundance of knowledge and wisdom. This is what is stated, "for the earth shall be full of the knowledge of the Lord as the waters cover the sea," and "for they shall see eye to eye, when the Lord returns to Zion, the glory of the Lord shall be revealed, and all flesh shall see it together." Then signs and wonders will not be necessary to verify the faith, but in terms of knowledge and comprehension, like all the prophets and angels who recognize God in terms of their comprehension, this is clear and true knowledge upon which no doubt will fall. Such was the comprehension of all Israel at Mount Sinai, as it is written, "The Lord spoke with you face to face at the mountain from the midst of the fire," and "for from the heavens I have spoken with you," and "so that the people may hear when I speak with you, and may also believe in you forever," that the faith should not be in terms of wonders, that if some doubt falls on the wonders themselves, the faith will be confused, but clear knowledge in terms of sight and comprehension, where there is no doubt at all.

Indeed, for the existence of man, there are elevations according to the elevation of his existence and its refinement, so will his comprehension and knowledge increase.

This is indeed the general principle of the gradation that God made for the attribute of His justice from its beginning to its completion. In the beginning, it is only fit to be destined to be done but is not done. After that, it is revealed a little, yet it is not called revealed, for things still need to be added to it that will testify to it, which are the wonders and miracles. When it is revealed in its signs, what is needed for the revelation of justice is completed, but in terms of what is external to it. There is also a completion of revelation in terms of itself, meaning in terms of knowledge and comprehension, that it itself will be comprehended. There are also additional revelations from it according to the elevation of existence of those who need to comprehend it.

I will show you a pleasant thing, how this entire gradation has an analogy in the world.

You will see the formation of man in its gradations. God was certainly able to give birth to man complete in all his perfection if He wanted, for He has no preventer. He did not do so, but man lacks much on the day of his birth and becomes more perfect little by little. You will find that he shows the glory of the Blessed One and His conduct in the revelation of His dominion, just as He conducts the world in the five states that we mentioned, which are the greatness of the world that grows like the growth of man, and the glory of the Omnipresent that is revealed in this great gradation.

The beginning of man's existence is through the union of his father and mother, who are the generators for every product. Indeed, he is closed in his mother's womb all the months of pregnancy. Afterwards, he is born and comes out to the air of the world, growing little by little. He is not yet complete, not in his stature nor in his mind, until he stands on his form. At first, he will be complete in his mind until he becomes obligated in commandments at thirteen years old. With all this, he is not yet complete and is still a youth. Afterwards, he will be complete and will fully stand on his feet. From then on, he has elevations upon elevations when he comes of age, in the splendor of old age, the crown of gray hair, the taste of elders, that many years will make known wisdom. All this is an analogy to the order of God's deeds in the gradation that we mentioned above. It is found that man himself, who is conducted by Him, shows in himself the conduct with which He conducts him.

Also, all the other creations of the world are so, each and every one an analogy to one of the secrets of His conduct. The supreme thought intended to make for all the orders of its conducts an analogy in this world. From here stems most of the multitude of creatures, that each and every creature shows one of the orders of His conduct. All the events of that creature are judged, in all its forms and properties, according to the matters of that order that stands to be shown in it, until all the attributes of God are found as if roots, and the creatures as branches to them literally, that the existence of these creatures depends on the existence of those attributes. From this already stemmed the visions of the prophets, that when God wanted to show them some of His attributes, in the prophetic image He showed them the lion, the ox, and all the other matters that came in the prophecies, and this is simple.

Let us now complete the matter that we are engaged in. According to what we explained, we find that for each and every attribute, there is the matter of that attribute and the power of that attribute, meaning the power of how it can reveal the matter that is in its law. The judgment is the principle of the ways of reward and punishment, whether for kindness or for His rod, included in three heads, which are the attribute of kindness, the attribute of justice, and the attribute of mercy. But the power of the revelation of this judgment according to its ways changes from time to time, and the revelation is found lacking or extra.

To what is this similar? To people whose image in all their limbs is equal, but the power is very different from one to another. Therefore, one will do what his fellow will not do, and in one person himself, there will be a difference in his power from one time to another, and this is simple. So is this matter, that God always conducts the world with this attribute of His judgment and fulfills all the laws of creation that depend on the ways of His judgment, but with more or less revelation, as we explained.

Here are found the differences between days in all the days of the year, that there are holy days and weekdays, and the difference between them is less or more revelation of His providence in the aspect of holiness, as we will further explain with the help of God.

The Changing Essence of the Lower Realms

Soul: There is certainly no end to wisdom, and to properly grasp matters, one needs much.

Intellect: But therefore it is said, "I said, 'I will be wise,' but it was far from me." Let us come to the matter. What emerges for us from all that we have spoken until now is that the Blessed Master, as you have already heard, is completely hidden from the comprehension of all His creatures, and His matter is not any of the matters that are grasped by our knowledge or depicted by our thought. Indeed, He wanted to bestow from Him some bestowals that relate and are suitable for us, for which we attribute to Him all His many descriptions and recount His praises according to our little strength alone.

This matter we have already explained above, that He innovated for His action and His providence some attributes and laws that we attribute to Him, like one who attributes the attributes and qualities to the soul. But we already know the great difference between these and the quality of the soul, for the soul is imprinted with those qualities, and they are a matter added to it over its essence, but with the Blessed Master, we do not imagine, God forbid, so, for we only know that with these attributes He acts, but not that these should be qualities imprinted in Him or accidents added to Him, God forbid, for we already know that He is devoid of all accident and of all that we distinguish in His creatures. We only mention these attributes of His from the side of what is done to us from His bestowal and His providence, but not that we understand how these divine attributes are in Him at all. This matter we have already explained in its place, and the unique one among the authors, the great Rabbi Maimonides of blessed memory, has already expanded to speak about this in his Guide book.

However, we certainly know that even these attributes that we distinguish in His action are only things innovated by Him for our need, according to our value and not at all according to His value. The principle of these attributes that He innovated for His action are the sources of all that is done at all times in His creatures. They are in the order of a superior conduct aimed at the purpose of perfecting all the creatures, all matters in gradation, one matter higher than another, up to the highest of all the matters included in these divine attributes. Indeed, the distinction of this gradation is only made from the actions, for when we gather all that is done by Him in His creatures, we define each thing according to its truth and evaluate all these actions one with the other, and we will find in them this value in that they are an action more honorable than an action, and therefore it is called higher than it.

We attribute the attributes to Him according to the actions that come from Him, and according to the order of the actions, we attribute the order and value to the attributes. It is found to the sages who understood the orders of the conduct, that they decreed the existence of these divine attributes, automatically the actions that follow from them, connecting one to the other in many ways and many matters. For even though each attribute is a matter in itself, the Blessed Master wanted and made all the attributes connect one to the other, until to complete the matter of one it will need the help of the other in that measure and part that is needed.

There is deep wisdom in the matter of this connection, to know the connection of all matters of the conduct, like the links of the chain that enter one into the other. Maimonides of blessed memory said in chapter 54 of his Guide part 1, "They said 'all My goodness' is a hint to show him all the existents, meaning, in showing them to him that he will comprehend their nature and their connection one to another." For behold, there are some of these attributes that will connect one to the other in the way of cause and effect, and in their connection will be distinguished all that needs to be attributed to the relation of the cause and its effect. There are some in the way of partnership to some matter in the way of help, much or little. There are some in the way of bestowal and reception, meaning that an innovation of some branch will emerge from one of the attributes, and that innovation will be received from the other.

I will give you an analogy to the matter of a person who contemplates some thing that he sees and wants to comprehend its matter. At first, the power of depiction will be used in it, to depict that thing in his mind. Indeed, if he does not use the other power, he will only make the depiction in his mind. But if he wants to understand it, the power of contemplation will be aroused in him, and he will take the thing in it, divide it, dissect it, again combine its parts, to separate what needs to be separated and to combine what needs to be combined, until he takes from it a complete knowledge. All these are things that certainly need to be done in the soul of a person before he comprehends the desired matter, even though these actions are not physical but spiritual, but they need to be done. Here we found that the subject depicted in the depicting power will emerge from it and will be given to the power of contemplation to do with it its own, as we explained. This is a connection of attributes in the way of bestowal and reception, and this is simple. It is found in the orders of the conduct that each lower level is caused by the level above it and also needs it, until to complete the matters of the lower level itself, some measure of what will enter from the upper level itself will enter in a hidden way. We will distinguish for the lower level itself a near cause and a far cause. All this is for the great precision of the estimation, that everything is estimated with ultimate deep wisdom.

You will see that this is what the Blessed Master did for Israel at Mount Sinai, for He did not give them there the entire Torah at that assembly, but it was a general preparation for all the service of the commandments. Then He first perfected for them all the crowns and levels fitting for a man made to serve his Maker, that at first his level was lowered to be prone to the evil inclination, as we explained, and then he was compared to the animals. When they came to Mount Sinai, the Blessed Master gave them all the preciousness that reaches them to be perfected in their existence, to have the power to be His servants.

Then He brought them close to Him with love, which is the matter of "He brought us near before Mount Sinai," so what we say every day, "And You brought us near to Your great Name" etc. He attached them to Him with His love, and then He first gave them the power to keep all His commandments, that their deeds in His service will make the good fruit necessary for the correction of the entire creation. It is what is written, "And you shall be to Me a kingdom of priests and a holy nation." From then on, Israel remained separated from the nations, crowned with supreme power to keep all the commandments, to correct with them the entire creation, as we explained. This thing is innovated always, and it does not cease from Israel, like the matter that is stated, "This day you have become a people" etc. - that a person is obligated to see himself as if he is receiving the Torah from Mount Sinai, for all this praise is innovated for Israel each and every day, each thing in its time.

Partnership Between the Righteous and God

Let us now explain the existence of the partnership that we mentioned between the righteous and the Holy One, Blessed be He, in the correction of the creation. The Blessed Master innovated the existence of the darkness imprinted in the lower ones in which the existence of evil depends, also its passing and its return to good, as we explained. He bestows to the lower ones only according to their preparation, and therefore it is relevant to the righteous to be going and correcting little by little this dark nature that we mentioned, for according to what they will correct in it, so the Blessed Master will bestow new superior bestowals, according to the value of the preparation and correction done in the nature of the lower ones. Therefore, the righteous offer before the Blessed Master an existence of new preparation and new correction in the dark nature that we mentioned, and the Holy One, Blessed be He, will answer them with a superior bestowal according to the value of that preparation. It is proper for the righteous to increase in the existence of the lower ones preparation upon preparation and correction upon correction, and in relation to them, the Blessed Master will bestow bestowal upon bestowal with an addition of elevation upon elevation.

After the sin of Adam, the world descended a great descent, as we explained, and lack was added upon lack in the existence of the lower ones. Therefore, what is needed now is to first correct the added lacks. This thing goes and is done until the time of the redemption, for this is the ultimate intention in the exiles, to correct what was corrupted and to gain what we lacked, in order to afterwards attain the good that will come to us afterwards, as it would have been fitting to come to Adam the first if he had not sinned, as we explained above. With the perfection of this matter, then we will be redeemed with a complete redemption. It is found that we need to distance the evil from the boundary that was widened for it after the sin, as we explained, and to return the good things that we lost. According to what is always innovated from this matter from the deeds of the righteous in the preparation of the lower ones, so the Blessed Master bestows to them.

The Holy One, blessed be He, apportions from the essence of His conduct to the congregation of Israel, for it to be a partner with Him in completing the creation, that He will correct from one side and it from the other side, and from Him and from it the complete correction will be finished. In this aspect, our Sages said in the Midrash, "My dove, My perfect one" - "My twin." We find in the verse the matter of combining the bestowal and the reception for the completion of the existents, as it says, "My hand has laid the foundation of the earth, and My right hand has spread out the heavens; when I call to them, they stand up together," for the heavens influence and the earth receives, and nevertheless both are balanced, this like that, by the completion of existence from between the two. Therefore, they said in the aforementioned Midrash, "Nevertheless, I am not greater than it, and it is not greater than Me." Indeed, the matter of influence is compared to the right, for it is the dominant one, and the need and reception to the left, which is lower than the right.

Behold, you have already heard how all matters of the lower realms are dependent on speech, and therefore the root of all these matters is the existence of a supernal power that sustains them in all their states. The matters of this power are equated and related to the matters of His blessed influences in all their orders, and as I have explained to you above in the explanation of the verse, "You shall see My back, but My face shall not be seen," for the kinds of influences are those by which the closeness or distance between Israel and their Father in Heaven is estimated, and according to the relation and equation of the power of the lower realms with the kinds of His blessed influences, the state of the lower realms will change in all their matters, for I have already informed you how they are all one bundle, branches of one tree alone.

Soul: Certainly this is a reasonable explanation, that in the changing essence of the lower realms from state to state there will be things within, meaning some changing source, that according to its changing flavor the results seen in the lower realms will change, and its change will be equated to the change of the kinds of influence.

Intellect: There is still a place of discernment for us in what is between this power and the lower realms themselves; meaning, for man is built of body and soul, and we know that all the movements of the body are born from the soul. However, we must also know how the soul settles in the body itself, and how it acts in it to produce those movements in the body, so we must also know the matters of the power of the lower realms with the lower realms themselves.

I will inform you of a profound matter in this, which is that the supernal glory dwells in every place, and it is what enlivens all existence, and Scripture attested, "You enliven them all," and therefore it is said, "The whole earth is full of His glory." However, the sins of man distance the glory from the lower realms, and this is the matter of which it is said, "But your iniquities have separated between you and your God." Conversely, merits cause the glory to dwell in the lower realms, and this is the matter of "Let them make Me a sanctuary, that I may dwell among them." Behold, the glory itself is exalted and elevated in its dwelling in the lower realms. The Sages have already said, "Everything that the Holy One, blessed be He, created in His world, He did not create but for His glory." Regarding the exile it is said, "They went without strength before the pursuer," for the supernal power was distant from them, and like the matter of "their defense is removed from over them." Regarding the redemption of Israel it is said, "Arise, shine, for your light has come, and the glory of the Lord has shone upon you," and then the glory itself will be exalted, and this is simple.

You should know that this matter is very necessary for understanding the angels and their actions. The Master, blessed be He, wanted to do His deeds through servants - His holy angels. Therefore, He wanted His Presence to dwell upon these angels, His emissaries who carry out all His decrees. His mastery is always with them, as the Sages said (Yalkut Shimoni II, 797),

"'The Lord is with them' - His mastery is with them." They also said (Tanchuma Mishpatim 18), "The name of the Holy One, blessed be He, is shared with each and every angel." This glory stands over all the hosts and cleaves to them always, but in proportion to the angel and its importance, for they too are enumerated in levels, each according to its value.

You should further know that even though the glory is in every place, it is nevertheless revealed more in one place than another. This designated place is where those who wish to cleave to it will seek it, as it is written (Deuteronomy 12:5), "But unto the place which the Lord your God shall choose out of all your tribes to put His name there, even unto His habitation shall you seek, and there you shall come." It is also written (Exodus 34:23), "Three times in the year shall all your males appear before the Lord God, the God of Israel."

Many orders and arrangements in great gradation are required to reach and cleave to His holiness. The entire structure of the Tabernacle and the Temple is based on this, with place within place, until the Holy of Holies where the glory dwells to be sought and found by those who seek to cleave to it. There is a Temple above corresponding to the Temple below (Tanchuma and Pesikta Zutra Mishpatim 18). All the host above praises this glory, saying (Isaiah 6:3), "Holy, holy, holy, is the Lord of hosts; the whole earth is full of His glory," and (Ezekiel 3:12), "Blessed be the glory of the Lord from His place," for He alone is the power of all existence, as we have explained. Thus it is said (Psalms 104:31), "May the glory of the Lord endure forever; the Lord will rejoice in His works," for the glory is exalted from the praise of His works. For this the Sages said (Chullin 60a), "This verse - the ruler of the world said it."

The exaltation of the glory is made from the power of all existences, each according to its kind and the action designated for it. This was the intention of the priest in performing the sacrificial service, particularly the daily offering, of which it is said (Numbers 28:2), "My offering, My bread." They offer this before Him, may He be blessed, every day for the benefit of all existences. The priest intended to elevate the glory of the Omnipresent, blessed be He, by gathering all the kinds in existence, each one according to what pertains to it. This required great wisdom that the priests needed to approach the Lord, on behalf of all Israel, and make their service truly desirable.

Therefore it is said (Malachi 2:7), "For the priest's lips should keep knowledge, and they should seek the law at his mouth," etc. They intended to bind all creatures to the Creator, and know what is necessary to complete this matter, intending all the necessary details - the orders of the service in all matters of the offering, such as the sprinkling of the blood and the burning of the incense. All were made for profound secrets to complete all existences in their attachment to the Creator. The explanation of this matter is extensive, but this is not its place.

The general intention is to bind all existences, the lower ones and the upper ones above them, all to the supernal glory, of which it is said (Jeremiah 23:24), "Do I not fill heaven and earth?" This is done through those orders arranged for this purpose, like servants gathering under the shade of their master.

However, the righteous have a particular service given over to their hands, as we have explained. Their task is to complete the repair of creation itself by preparing each day a new repair in what pertains to them, so that the Master, blessed be He, will correspondingly bestow an influence of blessing according to their arousal and preparation.

All the deficiencies in creation result from the concealment of His perfection and unity. When His unity rules, it acts to repair creation completely and remove every impediment that separates between the creatures and the Creator, as we said regarding the verse (Isaiah 59:2), "But your iniquities have separated," etc. When the righteous perform this service, the supernal unity is aroused, and some revelation of it is revealed according to the preparation of that service. This adds an additional repair in the entire creation according to the value of that service, for there is no service that does not add repair to the world by revealing His unity, which removes what separates between the creatures and the Creator, and attaches the creatures to the supernal glory. The existence of the lower realms cleaves to His holiness, in all the ways that He arranged for His holiness to emanate upon them - the kinds of His influences, which are all kinds of blessing that He, may He be blessed, blesses His creatures with.

Initially, the attachment of the souls to His holiness, strengthens, like a part that cleaves to its whole, as Scripture compared (Deuteronomy 32:9), "For the portion of the Lord is

His people." It is explained at the beginning of the Song of Songs (1:2), "Let him kiss me with the kisses of his mouth," showing the intensity of the attachment. This is a kind of strong attachment that can be made between the Holy One, blessed be He, and the Assembly of Israel, analogous to a kiss in man. Out of the intensity of the attachment, the Holy One, blessed be He, bestows upon the Assembly of Israel and all His creatures an influence of holiness - a G-dly and spiritual influence, and an influence of blessing, which is an influence for success even in this world. When the lower realms cleave to Him, may He be blessed, with the attachment of love, the Holy One, blessed be He, arouses love between Himself and them, and desires their service. This is like what the Sages established: "Who chooses His people Israel with love," and "May it be the will before You, Lord our God, that You find favor in Your people Israel and their prayer." It is from the aspect of this will that their service is effective in repairing creation, as we have explained above. Only the power of the supernal command and will makes the deed of the commandments beneficial and repairing. From the power of this will, the service is effective for what it is meant to be effective for, and the influence of blessing is bestowed in all the ways arranged for this matter.

The blessing is renewed in the entirety of the lower realms, and afterwards it reaches individuals, each one as befits him. These are His ways, the ways of the Lord are right, to deal with the lower realms for their benefit and their good. One who delves into them will find good reason and knowledge, delving and elevating in the entire Torah and its commandments, not one of them missing.

The Service of the Righteous and Israel

I will inform you of another fundamental matter. The Assembly of Israel has a root of holiness, general to the entire holy nation from the aspect of their being Israel, even to the wicked among them. The Sages said (Sanhedrin 44a), "Even though he sinned, he is [still] Israel." Even though this matter is rooted in very lofty matters, in Israel being descended from Him, may He be blessed, as Scripture said (Lamentations 3:24), "The Lord is my portion, says my soul; therefore I will hope in Him," the governance of the many and very broad worlds in all the orders of existences for good or for bad is not dependent on this, but on the deeds of those people, judging each one according to his deeds.

It is found that the Assembly of Israel has a general existence that does not have many results and branches. It is an existence that is not so fundamental, even though it is very lofty. Its fundamental existence is according to the service in its hand, upon which all matters of the great and profound governance depend.

You should also know that the matter of the day and the week is one cycle that goes and cycles, as we will explain below with the help of God. The main part of the week is the Sabbath, and the rest of the week is nothing but the completion of what is dependent on the Sabbath itself. An influence is renewed on the Sabbath, and on the rest of the days of the week that influence produces its results for what is needed for all existences each day according to its measure and the orders of the cycle. The main part of the day is the morning, and its other times are the completion of the matter that is renewed in the morning.

However, the lower realms draw down the main influence according to their main aspect, and the rest of the non-primary matters of influence are drawn according to the non-fundamental matter of the lower realms. This is simple, for everything goes in correspondence and equation - the influence with its recipients, and the actions with those acted upon.

You will understand that the Master, blessed be He, Who is exalted and lofty and not comprehended at all, innovated kinds of holiness that emanate from Him, may He be blessed, to the lower realms. Even this holiness is not like the matter of His essential holiness, hidden and incomprehensible, but rather it is equated to the preparation of its recipients. Even in this, gradation occurs, for there can be a holiness greater than another holiness, lesser holy things, and holy of holies. This is simple.

The Master, blessed be He, constantly innovates new repairs in the entirety of creation according to the arousal of the lower realms, as we have explained. In each repair, all the conditions necessary for its completion and for the completion of all the results that need to be born from it are required. All this is done when the creatures cleave to Him.
However, for the innovation of one of the main repairs, the cleaving of the creatures is required, and the main one - the

Assembly of Israel, in the aspect of the main part of their existence, in their most honorable aspect upon which all of existence depends. Then they draw down from Him a great and fundamental influence required for that repair innovated through them. But for the completion of the matters of that repair, cleaving is not required except in their aspects equated to the value of those conditions completed in it. This is simple according to the reason of correspondence and gradation.

All these matters the priests who offered the offering of the Lord needed to know - the daily offerings according to their order and the additional offerings according to their law, according to the distinctions of the times, as we have explained. They needed to know the level of the cleaving of the creatures, which revelation of the supernal will would be revealed, and which influence would be drawn down to them, all according to the time and the need of the hour.

Until here the Lord has helped me to explain to you what you need for the governance of reward and punishment. Now let us explain the second governance that we mentioned, the concealed governance that goes to the ultimate goal of the general perfection. Here the matter of "Everything depends on mazal," which the Sages mentioned (Zohar Nasso 134a), will be explained.

Soul: You have mentioned to me a matter that I greatly desire to understand, for it is one of the most difficult matters for me. Therefore, I very much desire to know its resolution.

Intellect: But here is found the matter of "the righteous to whom good happens, the righteous to whom bad happens," which is not given to be known.

Soul: If so, why did you arouse me about it, since you cannot explain it?

Intellect: There is a boundary to the matter up to where we understand, after which we cease to investigate. I will inform you of what is sufficient for us to settle the matter by seeing its fairness, and what is not given to be known - we will not seek. But you will see that what cannot be comprehended does not confuse the faith at all and does not muddle the ideas. You will see that it is nothing but additional knowledge that is not compulsory for us. But the clarification required for settling the heart and for clarifying the faith - we certainly have. The Lord God did not do anything that people should err in their faith, that they should not find its resolution. Therefore it is said (Deuteronomy 4:39), "Know therefore this day, and consider it in your heart, that the Lord He is God," etc.
Soul: If so, say what you know to be necessary for me.

Intellect: Since the Master, blessed be He, placed the governance of reward and punishment, from now on each person receives according to his deeds - good to the good and bad to the bad. However, the profound counsel of the Master, blessed be He, is to revolve matters in a way that the governance will be only for good, and there will be no existence of evil at all in the world. This is called the complete repair of the governance itself and its refinement.

In order to make this general repair, it is necessary to conduct Himself according to the root of the existence of good and evil. One who wants to heal an illness completely needs to uproot the cause, and then the effect will cease. So too in this matter, in order to make the governance only for good with no existence of evil, it is necessary to know the cause that currently brings about the existence of evil in the governance. According to that cause, it will be necessary to revolve the matters in a way that will produce this fruit - that there will no longer be evil in the governance. This is simple, for the Holy One, blessed be He, does not want to change His mind, like a person who regrets his first deeds and leaves one way for another. Rather, according to the first foundation itself, He will revolve the matters to come to the perfection that He wants.

The root of the existence of evil in the governance, as we have explained, is because of the revelation of His unity, that it is necessary to reveal the evil and let it do all that is in its law, to show afterwards the unity of His dominion, may He be blessed, in turning it back to good. For this reason, as long as the Master, blessed be He, conceals and hides His face, and lets the evil grow stronger up to the furthest boundary that it can grow stronger (meaning up to the destruction of the world, but not including it), this will be more of a reason for the truth of His unity, to be revealed and seen afterwards, in His repairing those corruptions with the power of His dominion. The light is recognized from within the darkness, as we have explained above.

Therefore, when the Master, blessed be He, wants to establish the governance of the world for good, He needs to arrange His governance according to this root matter of the revelation of unity that we mentioned, from which the current existence of good and evil is born.

Reward and punishment does not strengthen evil, for in any case there is no evil except to the evil, and those who forsake the Lord will perish, but those who seek Him - He will be sought by them. The strengthening of evil is when the Holy One, blessed be He, completely hides His face from His world, of which it is said (Proverbs 1:28), "Then they will call upon Me, but I will not answer," and (Isaiah 29:15), "The truth is lacking, and he who departs from evil is considered foolish." This is called the complete concealment that is done only in order to reveal afterwards a complete repair, as Scripture said (Isaiah 59:16), "His arm saved for Him, and His righteousness sustained Him." According to this order and governance, they do not pay attention to merit or liability, but the governance conducts itself according to its orders, meaning, to let the evil have the great upper hand in order to show afterwards the dominion of good.

As long as evil has the upper hand, even the good will need to stand under the affliction of evil, not because the judgment is so, but because the time requires it. Afterwards they will receive a complete reward when the good returns, is revealed and rules, according to the evil that they suffered at first, as it is written (Psalms 90:15), "Make us glad according to the days You have afflicted us," etc. But as long as evil has the upper hand, their merit will not avail them to be saved from it, like the verse (Amos 5:13), "Therefore the prudent shall keep silence in that time; for it is an evil time." Not only that, but since it is the nature of evil that all corruption and destruction of order occur, not only will merit not avail the righteous to be saved from the evil, but on the contrary, people of evil will succeed, and the time will laugh at them. The upright are afflicted and oppressed, as the Sages said (Sotah 49b), "In the footsteps of the Messiah, brazenness will increase, etc., the wisdom of the scribes will become spoiled," etc. Scripture itself says (Isaiah 59:15), "The truth is lacking, and he who departs from evil is considered foolish," etc.

It is found that if the Master, blessed be He, wants to conduct the world according to the governance of unity - to recognize the light from within the darkness and to make it so that the evil itself will turn back to good - He will need to give the upper hand to evil without paying attention to the merit of the righteous. On the contrary, then the doers of wickedness will be built up, and the righteous - their head will be lowered to the dust.

After this He will reveal His dominion, and the fruit of the revelation will be to turn the evil itself back to good, and there will no longer be evil in the world, only good. Then the righteous will receive their reward, and not before that. But if He conducts [the world] according to reward and punishment, then there will be only good to the good and bad to the bad, but there is nothing here that will bring about a complete repair of the governance that will nullify the existence of evil, for why should it be nullified when it is only for the evil, and it is limited in its boundary to not do according to its evil nature but according to the proper law.

Since the Holy One, blessed be He, truly wants the complete repair of the world and the complete nullification of evil, therefore He wants to go with the righteous in the way of the governance of unity that we mentioned, that their righteousness will not avail them to save them from the sufferings of this world. This is certainly not because of reward and punishment, but rather in order that the complete repair will be repaired through them. This is certainly good for them, for then they will receive a greater reward than they would have received according to their bare merit. But it is also good for the world, for if He would conduct Himself with them according to reward and punishment, no fruit would come out of their good deeds except the reward of their deeds, but not the removal of evil from the world. But since what they suffer is not because of their deeds but because of the order of the governance, therefore also the benefit will not be particular to them to give them reward, but general to the governance, to reveal through their merit the supernal unity, and the evil will be nullified from the governance itself.

You will see how an additional benefit is added with this - that even the revelation of the supernal dominion will be with merit and not entirely with charity. Even though it is with charity in relation to the rest of mankind, but in relation to the righteous it is with merit, and from their good He will do good to the entire world, and the whole Assembly of Israel is found meritorious.

Soul: However, if so, it would have been proper that all the righteous would be nothing but afflicted, and reality is not so.

Intellect: This matter has a very profound root. This is, that the Master, blessed be He, made the evil with that constitution that He made it, and with those boundaries that He wanted it. He revolves revolutions to completely remove it from the creation, as we have explained. However, He needs to revolve these revolutions according to the matter of evil, and according to the orders that He made it, and this is simple.
After the Master, blessed be He, made this creation lacking perfection, He revolves these revolutions to complete it by removing its deficiencies. He, may He be blessed, alone knows the root of all the matters that He wanted to make, and the reasons for all His decrees that are hidden from His creatures, for the creatures know only from the decrees of the supernal will and onward, but above this, meaning, the reasons for these decrees, in truth were not given over to the creatures at all, and they are the forbidden investigations for us, for the matters are rooted in the loftiness of the will that wants them, which is impossible for us to comprehend.
Behold, He, may He be blessed, knows that to complete this creation, two things are needed: the intensification of the illumination, meaning the intensification and abundance of the

influence, and its concealment and diminishment. There are matters that are repaired with an abundance of illumination and influence, and there are matters that are repaired on the contrary with concealment and diminishment, by letting the evil have the great upper hand, as we have explained.

This matter will be seen clearly to one who pays attention to everything that is born in the world, for he will find that nothing is born, not for good and not for bad, that benefit and good to the world will not result from it. They have already said (Berachot 60b), everything that they do from heaven is for good. However, the place has many ways, these to the right and these to the left, and these matters do not depend on deed and merit, but on the constitution and essence of creation. He, may He be blessed, Who alone knows the true essence of creation, also knows what is required for it.

We only know this: that in the essence of creation, for its completion, abundance and diminishment are needed. It is the matter of the 28 times mentioned in the book of Ecclesiastes (chapter 3), corresponding to which the moon in the sky waxes and wanes to be an analogy to this matter.

The wise have profound knowledge in this matter in understanding the ways of the moon and its paths, and its conjunction with the sun in all its occurrences, which are an exact analogy to all the general matters of the governance that surrounds to complete the creation according to this constitution that it has, as we have explained, that for the completion of its matter, abundance and diminishment are needed, for which reason they compared the Assembly of Israel to the moon, and said (Sanhedrin 42a), "that they are destined to be renewed like it." The details in this matter are many and profound. But the general matter is, that the cycle that surrounds Israel and all creatures to complete their repair from the aspect of the constitution of creation, not from the aspect of the deed of the lower realms - all its matters are seen in this moon and everything discerned in it.

Indeed, the Master, blessed be He, divided the general repair of creation among all the souls that He made to serve Him, according to what He knew to be fitting for each of them according to the matter that He created it, which is a matter that is very, very hidden, and was not comprehended by any prophet or seer, for all this is included in the reasons of the decrees that we mentioned, which are hidden from the creatures, and only the results will be known to us.

It is found, that there is a person who it befalls him from the aspect of the root of his matter to be influenced with an abundance of influence, which is one of the ways in which the creation is completed as we have explained, and there is a person who it befalls him from the aspect of the root of his matter to be influenced with a diminishment of influence, which is the second way that is required for the completion of creation. This is not because of the deeds of those people, but because of what befalls them according to how the Master, blessed be He, divided the repair of creation among the creatures, for this is a repair for it and this is a repair for it, each one according to its way.

Indeed, the judgment belongs to God, to afterwards give a good reward to the righteous, who were righteous and it befell them because of the ways of the supernal governance to be afflicted and tortured because of the affliction that they had in this world, and corresponding to all their good deeds. Indeed, the Sages called this entire governance that does not turn to merit and liability, but its turning is to what is required for the completion of creation according to its essence, "mazal," since its matter is nothing but a decree, and it does not depend on the choice of man and his merit. However, I have already said, this matter only conducts itself in this world, but in the World to Come there is nothing but the reward of deeds, measure for measure, even the reward for a nice statement.

Soul: However, if so, it is decreed that there is no reward and punishment in this world at all, but [only] in the World to Come? Intellect: It is not so; but you need to know a fundamental introduction, and it is, that the Sages said (Bereishit Rabbah 25:3), "There was a famine in the days of David' (II Samuel 21:1) - the essence of that calamity was not fit to be in the days of David, but in the days of Saul, but since Saul was [swept away as] a sycamore beam, the Holy One, blessed be He, revolved it and brought it in the days of David." So they said (Bereishit Rabbah 55:2), "This flax dealer, when he inspects his flax, he only inspects it, etc." You have before you that the Master, blessed be He, does not always use this governance of mazal that we mentioned, but [only] at a time that He knows that it is good to use it. The Master, blessed be He, prepared profound orders in the completion of creation, as we have explained, and made for Himself two ways, the way of reward and punishment and the way of mazal, and He is the One Who chooses, and uses sometimes the one way and sometimes the other way, what He knows to be better for His world. However, when He uses the way of reward and punishment - all the matters that are born will be according to the orders of reward and punishment in their laws; and when He uses the way of mazal - the matters that are born will be according to the order of the governance of mazal and the constitution of creation, as we have explained.

Behold, this too will generate more merit for the righteous, for if the Master, blessed be He, would always afflict specifically the righteous - it would be a trial, but not so very great, for in any case they would console themselves to know that they are certainly righteous, since they are afflicted; and every rational person would choose these sufferings, for they are certainly only the sufferings of the righteous, for the wicked are not afflicted. However, the Master, blessed be He, wanted there to be a place for an even greater trial, that people should not be able to clearly understand what the Holy One, blessed be He, does in the world with each and every person. But what will appear at first glance - is that "All things come alike to all; there is one event to the righteous and to the wicked" (Ecclesiastes 9:2).

The Sages explained this matter in the Midrash (Yalkut Shimoni, Ecclesiastes 989, and see there in the section before it), Solomon looks at all the generations and sees things that happen to the wicked happen to the righteous," etc. Meaning, for the Holy One, blessed be He, will see that the same occurrence that will be born to a wicked person who will transgress one of the transgressions in particular, and that punishment will be related to that transgression, will also be born to righteous people who will be very, very careful with that same transgression; and that is, Abraham and Nimrod, and all the others mentioned in the Midrash there, for the reality proves this truth that it is certainly so.

This is done in order to give an even better reward to the righteous who strengthen themselves in their faith, and it is what Scripture said (Habakkuk 2:4), "But the righteous shall live by his faith." It is impossible for any person to stand on the clarification of the things that the Holy One, blessed be He, does with him, for He, may He be blessed, conducts Himself sometimes in the way of reward and punishment and sometimes in the way of mazal, as we have explained. With each and every thing that renews itself upon a person, There is no one there who will judge whether it is from reward and punishment, and according to his deeds, or from the mazal that decrees upon him; and in each and every thing there are aspects this way and that way, until the heart storms greatly from its many thoughts and contemplations within it. But one who is faithful to the Lord, needs to drive the stake of his faith strongly so that it will not fall, to know that all the deeds of the Lord, in whatever way they may be, are certainly fair and faithful, and there is no injustice, God forbid, and not like the wicked who would say, the way of the Lord is not proper; but upon his watch he will stand to serve his Creator with complete service, with one equanimity in every measure that He measures to him, and then he will truly be called perfect.

The general principle - there are two ways, the way of reward and punishment and the way of mazal; and the Master, blessed be He, uses them according to what He knows to be good for His world. In the Midrash of Rabbi Shimon bar Yochai, one statement is found, that even though its matter is profound in the secrets of the attributes, but its surface appears very strange to one who does not know these introductions that I have informed you. This is the language of the statement (Tikkunei Zohar, Tikkun 70), "At a time when the Lord removes Himself from the Throne of Judgment and from the Throne of Mercy, there is there neither reward nor punishment," for it seems as if, God forbid, there is no reward and punishment. However, the true intention is to inform us that there is a time that the Master, blessed be He, does not conduct the world with the governance of reward and punishment, but with the governance of mazal, and as we have explained, that good and bad are drawn down and come according to the matters of the governance for the need of the general repair.

Reward and Punishment will be for the World to Come

Intellect: But certainly the reward and punishment will be for the World to Come, to give to a man according to his ways and according to the fruit of his deeds. However, it informs us, that at the time of the height of the footsteps of the Messiah, it should not be difficult for us if the righteous are very greatly lowered, and if people cry out and are not answered, and all the other bad things that the Sages said (Sotah 49b), "In the footsteps of the Messiah brazenness will increase," for all this is born because the righteous are not able even with their merit to repair those corruptions, for the time causes so, and in order to generate from this the complete repair that will be afterwards with the revelation of His unity, and as we have explained.

Indeed, you need to know an introduction, which we need a lot to settle many doubts. It is, that even at a time when the Master, blessed be He, wants to conduct His world with the governance of mazal that we mentioned, behold, He turns and causes the matters, that even what needs to come according to mazal - will come from within the ways of the governance of reward and punishment. We found a matter like this [with] the sufferings of Rebbi, for the Sages said (Bava Metzia 85a), "They came because of an incident and they left because of an incident." In truth those sufferings were only from the sufferings of the righteous, but such is the attribute, that the Holy One, blessed be He, combines these two governances together, and even the decrees of mazal will not come except through some matter that relates to reward and punishment that they can depend on, for through it will revolve everything that needs to revolve, even though in itself it will be only a small thing. The general principle - the root of the governance in truth is the matter of the general repair of all existence, which cycles on the poles of the constitution of existence itself, according to what the Creator, made them; and all the revolutions of this governance are only the cycles of matters that go to the ultimate purpose of this general repair that we mentioned, in removing from them all the deficiencies that exist in them. This matter has profound laws and orders that are not comprehended at all. While these revolutions revolve and go, there is the governance of reward and punishment, which is the revealed governance, that all the laws of heaven and earth depend on it.

However, the inwardness of all the orders and laws are bound with the matter of the general repair that we mentioned, for they are not two opposite and contradictory governances, but on the contrary, the main one is the governance of the general repair; but the Master, blessed be He, knew in His lofty wisdom, to arrange proper laws of reward and punishment to serve the entire time of the cycle of this governance, and they will be laws that relate and are suitable and equated in their inwardness to the revolutions of the governance of repair. Therefore the governance of reward and punishment will not go outside the center of the governance of the general repair, on the contrary, it is equated to it and joins with it, and the matters of the governance of repair itself will be drawn and come in the ways of reward and punishment, and as we have explained.

However, the Master, blessed be He, concealed from His creatures the comprehension of this supernal governance, and it and its matters, and the relation between it and the governance of reward and punishment are not revealed and known. No prophet or seer stood on the clarification of this matter, but they saw what they saw, and did not stand on its clarification, but rather always remained with many doubts, and as the Sages said regarding the verse (Exodus 33:19), "I will be gracious to whom I will be gracious, and will show mercy on whom I will show mercy" (see Berachot 7a).

You need to know that the fruit of the good deeds that the righteous do, is what they will enjoy from them in the World to Come in the world of reward, meaning eternity. Indeed, in the good deeds themselves there is the repair that they repair now in creation according to the order that it is arranged, and there is the reward of what is fitting for them to receive according to this repair that they repaired. Therefore, the Master, blessed be He, needs to take the deeds of people according to what they are, and to judge them according to the result that is truly born from them - according to what the Holy One, blessed be He, allowed people to repair in the entire creation. This matter needs to be decreed according to the matter of the essence of creation as the Master, blessed be He, made it, and according to all the discernments discerned in its constitution.

You should know that nothing is forgotten before His throne of glory, and nothing is hidden from His eye, in His judging this judgment; meaning, do not say since a matter became corrupted, and afterwards was repaired, only the repair will be remembered before Him, and the corruption that was is already forgotten; or the opposite, in a matter that was repaired and became corrupted its repair that was will not be remembered; it is not so, but there is no forgetfulness before His throne of glory. The result that comes out from the repair that comes after the corruption, or the repair that comes after another repair, or a repair that comes after two corruptions, is not the same, and so on endlessly, what the mouth cannot speak. According to the revolution of the entirety of existence, each deed needs to be judged according to the past, present and future, for the repair of the entirety of creation is only repaired from everything that will revolve in all the six thousand years, the time of this world.

The Master blessed be He, in His knowledge will judge each thing according to the three times that we mentioned, for the result of each deed is only according to what preceded it, and according to the present with it, and according to all that comes after it. After this entire judgment, a reward is established for it for the World to Come, a reward befitting it according to its deeds, and this is simple. Behold, on the great day of judgment, the Master, blessed be He, will spread out the garment before the eyes of every creature, of all that was done from the day that God created man on the earth until that day, and He will show the fairness of His judgment in each and every deed, small and great, and what was decreed upon it according to His true judgment for the time of receiving reward in the World to Come. Afterwards, the righteous will go out to receive their reward, each one according to his deeds.

Soul: I have certainly learned a lot, and I was at least able to consider some consideration to quiet my mind regarding the matter of His providence. I saw a great place for the service of man, and what it is and what its benefit is. I saw the results of time that renew in the mornings, how many sources they have, meaning, the attribute of His judgment, and the attribute of His mercy, the governance of mazal, and what the ultimate purpose is in all these. I understood the existence of man in this time, and his exaltation in the time that he will be exalted. I understood the matter of the coming of the Messiah and the resurrection of the dead and the world of reward, what they are and what they are based on. Above all - the strength of faith, to know that everything is from Him, may He be blessed, with profound counsel, nothing is by chance and not for naught, not small and not great, for everything is a wheel that returns in the world, revolving and going to give a general repair to all of existence, and the end of its revolution will be this general repair. I think that up to here are principles of wisdom, and the rest is explanation, to understand all the details in the world, each one under its category. It is enough for me that the roots should be in my hand, so that I should at least be settled in my faith with clarity.

Intellect: I still have to explain to you the matter of time that goes in a cycle equally over all individuals. We find in it differences in its parts because of time itself, meaning, not because of deeds that will be innovated in it, but because of the time period itself being so. It is what Ecclesiastes said (3:1), "To every thing there is a season, and a time to every purpose." This too certainly needs to have a proper root.

Soul: This too is a matter that is pleasant to know with clarity.

Intellect: See, the stars and constellations each influence a specific and particular thing in this lower world. One who is influenced by one star is not influenced by its fellow. All recipients always receive from their influencers in every place. However, besides this charge that they have, they have dominion and rule in the cycle of time, that each one rules in the hour and time that was decreed for it, and this is known. Indeed, there is a great difference between these two dominions, for the dominion that each of them has over the things specific to it, is a dominion that reaches the essence of the recipients, that their entire matter depends on them, and they are affected in the inwardness of their essence by the influence that they influence upon them. But the dominion of the cycle is a general dominion, that each ruler rules over the entire world, whether over the creatures specific to it, or over the creatures that are not specific. But on the other hand, that dominion is not a complete dominion over any one of them, and they only receive from it some affectation. The dominion will certainly make a noticeable impression on the creatures from the aspect of that dominion, for there is no deed among the deeds of God, may He be blessed, that will be for naught, but this is not the essential action of these stars. But their essential action is only what they act specifically on the creatures specific to them, and as we have explained.

Indeed, this is an analogy made to show matters that are loftier and more hidden. Meaning, for the Master, blessed be He, innovated many kinds of influences to bestow upon His creatures, specific influences for each creature as is fitting for it. Besides this, He decreed a cyclical cycle for all these kinds of influences, for them to rule in a cycle over the world, that the order of their dominion and action should be in the order of the cycle of time. Each day, one of the kinds of influences rules in the governance, and it is a general dominion over the entire creation, but its action in this dominion is not its main action that it does in the existences that specifically receive from it, but nevertheless, matters will be innovated in the entire creation according to the matter of that influence, a result of this dominion of it. On this too depends the holiness of the festival days from year to year, and all the other things that depend on time. However, it is necessary to discern the discernment that I mentioned, that there is a difference between the specific action of each influence at all times, and the cyclical action which is not so fundamental to reach the inwardness of the essence of the recipient.

In this way is the matter of the creation of man and all his times, for you have already heard that they correspond to the orders of the supernal influence. It is certainly so that in each of his times he will be conducted according to the orders of the influences to which that time corresponds, but not in the way of the results that are specifically born from those influences, but in the way of the preparations of his body and limbs in that order. Behold, I have told you what will suffice to settle your mind on the truth in these principles that you asked of me, and nothing more.

Prophecy - Its Nature and Way

Soul: There is one more matter that I desire to know from you, but it is not such a lengthy matter, and also not one of those that confound the thought in the absence of knowledge about it, like the matters that we mentioned until now; but it is something that I desire to stand upon with clarity.

Intellect: What is this matter?

Soul: The matter of prophecy, what is it, what is its way and what is its benefit?

Intellect: Prophecy is knowledge and comprehension that the Holy One, blessed be He, gives to the prophet from His glory. Indeed, you have already heard that the truth of His essence, and His perfection, what He is according to Himself - is not given to be comprehended by us at all, and they only comprehend Him from the aspect of His actions and from the aspect of the attributes that He established for Himself to govern the world, and as we have explained. They comprehend Him as beneficent and punishing, merciful, judging, enlivening, healing, and with all the other appellations that are attributed to Him from the aspect of His actions. He shows them all His influences in all their ways, and they see all their matters upon which depend all the laws of the heavens and the earth and all their hosts and all their details. Therefore they know the past and the future of what the Holy One, blessed be He, does in the world, for they comprehend Him grasping in one of the attributes, and they comprehend all the results that are born from this in all the creatures that will be, and they comprehend Him grasping in the attribute that He grasped, and in the attribute that He will grasp in all the details of this entire matter. But His simple essence they do not comprehend. Even this comprehension that they comprehend will not be with plain sight, but in a way specific to prophecy.

Soul: This is what I am seeking to know, how is this sight.

Intellect: It is an explicit verse (Hosea 12:11), "I have also spoken unto the prophets, and I have multiplied visions; and by the hand of the prophets I use similes." Regarding Moshe our teacher, peace be upon him, it is said (Numbers 12:8), "even manifestly, and not in dark speeches," so for others - in dark speeches. It explicitly says (ibid.), "I speak with him in a dream," and the Sages confirmed what they received (Berachot 57b), "A dream is one-sixtieth of prophecy." This is because permission was not given to the prophets to see the supernal glory as it is, but the glory that is revealed to them innovates in their hearts prophetic images, which will be like garments and riddles for the matters that are fit to reach their knowledge, and like all the other parables and riddles in the world. Indeed, their way of comprehension is not like human thought comprehends in the natural way; but it is a comprehension bestowed within them, and imprinted knowledge, in which doubt and the need for examination and the practice of proofs will not occur, but it will become clear to them without any doubt that the One revealing Himself to them and speaking with them is His glory, and He is the One innovating those prophetic images in their hearts.

Knowledge is imprinted in their hearts as well - that they comprehend the interpretation of the vision and the riddle, and they comprehend what the Master, blessed be He, wants to reveal to them. The Rambam of blessed memory wrote words like these in chapter 7 of Hilchot Yesodei HaTorah (halachah 3), this is his language, "The matters that they inform the prophets in the vision of prophecy - in the way of a parable they inform him, and immediately the interpretation of the parable in the vision of prophecy is imprinted in his heart, and he knows what it is."

You need to discern that there are parables of attributes and parables of results. Meaning, there are parables in which the supernal glory is likened according to His attributes and actions, and there are parables that liken the Actor and what is acted upon by Him, may He be blessed. For example, when the Master, blessed be He, wants to show His glory to a prophet as beneficent and merciful - He will appear to him as an elder, as the matter that is said (Daniel 7:9) "The Ancient of Days did sit," and when He wants to show him as mighty over His enemies - He will appear as a young man of war, and as the Sages said

(Mechilta Yitro 20:2), "He was revealed at the sea as a young man and revealed at Mount Sinai as an elder"; (Chagigah 14a), "for a young man is fitting for war and an elder is fitting for sitting." But the parables of actions are like the matter of the rod of almond of Jeremiah, and the boiling pot, Jacob's ladder, Ezekiel's scroll, Zechariah's ephah, and the golden candlestick. With the parables of attributes, when the supernal glory shows those images to the eyes of the prophet, he immediately comprehends the interpretation of that vision. But with the parables of actions it is possible for them to not comprehend them until they are explained to them, and as we found with the prophets (Zechariah 4:5), "Don't you know what these are? I said, No, my lord," and like the words of the Rambam of blessed memory there.

Behold, from what is possible to be in their visions - this is a multiplicity of images, and even opposites to each other in one moment. The Sages taught us this matter in Tractate Sofrim (6:2), this is what they said, "'The Lord spoke with you face to face' (Deuteronomy 5:4). 'Face' is two, 'to face' is two, Four faces of awe - for Scripture, intermediate ones - for Mishnah, laughing ones - for Talmud, cheerful ones - for Aggadah." So they said (Yalkut Shimoni, Yitro 286), "'I am the Lord your God' (Exodus 20:2) - Rabbi Chama bar Pappa said, the Holy One, blessed be He, showed them angry faces, cheerful faces, etc.

He said to them, even though you see all these images - I am the Lord your God." This is like the way they also said regarding speech. (Jerusalem Talmud Nedarim 3:2, and see there further things), "'You shall not uncover the nakedness of your brother's wife' (Leviticus 18:16)," "'her husband's brother shall go in unto her' (Deuteronomy 25:5)" - they were said in one utterance; "Remember" and "Keep" - they were said in one utterance (ibid., and see Rosh Hashanah 27a). The reason for this is clear, for since these images are not essential, but a created prophetic revelation, dependent on the will of the King Who speaks and it is, that these images should appear to the soul of the prophet. He can create images as He wants in whatever way He wants, and He does not need the laws of this physical nature, which are only made for bodies alone. However, this is certain that none of the words of the Lord are for naught, God forbid, but each and every image that He shows him, is only to inform him of one attribute of His attributes, or a matter of His attributes. When He wants to show him different matters, He will show him different images, even though they will intrinsically be opposites, for the purpose is no longer on the image that appears, but on what is understood by the prophet from within that image.

Soul: But the verse that is written (Deuteronomy 4:15), "for you saw no manner of form," is very difficult for me, for it is the opposite of all these things that you spoke.

Intellect: Even without this is it not difficult that the verses contradict each other? One verse says, "for you saw no manner of form," and another verse says (Numbers 12:8), "and the similitude of the Lord does he behold"; and it is written (Ezekiel 1:26), "and on the likeness of the throne was a likeness as the appearance of a man upon it above," and all similar to it.

Soul: You answer both of them.

Intellect: It is written (Isaiah 40:25), "To whom then will you liken Me, that I should be equal to him? says the Holy One," and so (Isaiah 40:18), "To whom then will you liken God? Or what likeness will you compare with Him?" The principle of this is, that it is certain that the Holy One, blessed be He, does not mislead the prophet, God forbid, but makes him wise and establishes him upon the truth. For the Holy One, blessed be He, to show him images in a place where on the contrary one needs to very much distance himself from an image, there is no greater obstacle than this. However, the truth is, that the soul of the prophet comprehends the truth with clarity.

This is because you have already heard that the comprehension and knowledge of the prophet is not like the natural comprehension and knowledge, but it is a comprehension imprinted and engraved in him, that he will find complete clarity in his knowledge without any doubt. This is a kind of knowledge that the natural human mind cannot estimate at all. According to this way - the soul of the prophet will comprehend every matter of prophecy according to its truth, meaning, it will become clear to it that the Master, blessed be He, is the One revealing Himself to it, and informing it of what He informs it; and it will also become clear to it that it is impossible for it to gaze at Him; not only with the gaze of the physical eye, but even with a soulful gaze, which is nothing but comprehension and understanding, for the soul cannot comprehend His matter. It will become clear to it that the glory that is revealed to it innovates in it a created prophetic image, from within which it receives the knowledge that it needs to receive, and this is (Hosea 12:11), "and by the hand of the prophets I use similes," which we brought above.

It is found, that the truth becomes clear to it with complete clarity, and it has no place to err, for the true knowledge is engraved in it to know all this truth. Behold, it will not comprehend the prophetic image except if at that very time it also comprehends that it is only a prophetic image, and not the essence of the Master, blessed be He.

Therefore, even though it is said, "and by the hand of the prophets I use similes," He always warns them, "To what likeness will you compare Him?" The prophet does not see an image without also seeing that it is only a prophetic image, and not essential, made for the understanding of the prophet, who cannot comprehend His simple essence, completely devoid of any image. So our teacher, peace be upon him, warns Israel (Deuteronomy 4:15), "for you saw no manner of form," for there he speaks of the simple essence of the Master, blessed be He, and he says to them, be very careful, for you have already comprehended the truth, and you saw that you saw no form in Him, may He be blessed, but you saw that on the contrary, because of His essence, being devoid of any form, therefore you did not comprehend Him, but only after He created for you the prophetic images. Scripture is slightly concise, but it is no more concise than the other verses, "To whom then will you liken Me, that I should be equal to him?" "To what likeness will you compare Him?" for Moshe our teacher, peace be upon him, speaks with Israel who saw all this truth, and he reminded them of what they truly saw.

Soul: You explained "for you saw no manner of form," but you did not explain "and the similitude of the Lord does he behold."

Intellect: Even that image that appears to the soul of the prophet will fittingly be called "the similitude of the Lord." It is, that the prophet has no doubt that the One revealing Himself to them disguised in that image is none other than the unique Master, blessed be He and blessed be His name, upon which they can affirm with a full mouth (Ezekiel 1:28), "This was the appearance of the likeness of the glory of the Lord," (Isaiah 6:1), "I saw the Lord." Behold, in their bestowed comprehension it will become clear to them that that image is an image innovated from the revelation upon them of the supernal glory, and that form is only the way through which they reach the comprehension of this revelation of His. To what is this similar? To one who sees his fellow from within a mirror, for even though the essence of his fellow is not within that mirror, what he sees is truly only his fellow, who appears to him from within his looking in the mirror. Another thing is also born from this, that if the mirror itself will be strange, the form of his fellow will appear strange in it, according to the matter of the mirror.

Indeed, the seer will not doubt that the body that he sees will not be the body of his fellow standing there, but he will know that when his fellow stands opposite that strange mirror, and he looks in that mirror, that form will be innovated to his eyes. So too is this matter, the prophet knows that the Master, blessed be He, is certainly the One revealing Himself to him in that vision, even though that vision is only what is innovated to the eyes of the prophet from the aspect of his soul itself, or whatever it may be that causes him to see that image. Therefore that image will fittingly be called "the similitude of the Lord," and it will be said about it, "and the similitude of the Lord does he behold."

Soul: But now it will be difficult for me that according to your words there is no difference between the prophecy of Moshe and the other prophets, for they all see this form, and they all see that He, may He be blessed, has no intrinsic form.

Intellect: Now I will tell you a great difference between Moshe our teacher, peace be upon him, and the other prophets. The other prophets - even this image they cannot gaze at with a complete gaze, for it does not appear to them except as if from behind walls, or several mirrors, or an unclear vision. The Sages explained this matter on this very verse (Midrash Rabbah, Parashat Vayikra, 1:14), this is what they said, "What is the difference between Moshe and the other prophets? Rabbi Yehudah says, all the prophets saw from within nine mirrors, etc., and Moshe from within one mirror; and the Sages say, all the prophets saw from within a dim mirror, etc. and Moshe from within a polished mirror."

Since they cannot even properly see that image that appears to them, they do not comprehend the end of its matters, and automatically understanding will also be lacking for them from the interpretation, and this is simple; the Holy One, blessed be He, only shows them these images to inform them of knowledge included in that prophetic image, that in their seeing the image they will comprehend the knowledge included in it in all its parts; and if they comprehend the image itself only partially, it is certain that the complete knowledge will not reach them in all its parts, but only the part corresponding to the part that they saw of the image.

However, Moshe, at least the prophetic image he comprehended with clarity, and therefore his knowledge was complete in what is possible to be the knowledge of creatures, and he reached the degree of being the greatest of those with prophetic knowledge. But he too only saw what he was given permission to see, and this is simple.

Indeed, I will further alert you to one matter in this vision of prophecy, and it is, that even though we find that the prophets see these prophetic images, it is not necessary for them to see them with a sight like the sight of the physical eye, but with a soulful sight. One subject itself can be seen from the physical eye and from the soul divested of a body, and both of them will affirm it being that subject.

However, each one sees it according to its way, each one as it is, for the soul can see what is in a barrel and what is inside a wall, which is impossible for the physical eye because of its way of sight, for it can only reach what it can according to the boundary that the Creator, may He be blessed, placed for it. But the barrel itself the physical eye will see in its ways, and affirm it being a barrel, and the soul will see it in its ways, and also affirm it being a barrel. So too is this matter, that the prophets do not need to see the form that they will call "lion," and the form that they will call "eagle" (see Ezekiel 10:14), and so all similar to this, as the eyes of flesh would see that form, but in the way of soulful sight, and this is simple.

Soul: I still need to know, what need is there for these images? What would be lacking if the Holy One, blessed be He, would inform what He wants to inform of the knowledge or the future without them seeing any image at all?

Intellect: I can answer you in an easy and simple way, and it is, that the Holy One, blessed be He, wants to be revealed upon people in the ways of people, and as we have already explained. The creatures in their form itself show the supernal influences and attributes, and they are an exact analogy to them. Therefore, the Master, blessed be He, shows them His glory in the likeness of the creature created from Him, for that form below is nothing but an analogy of that influence and attribute that is above.

You will see, that this too is an attribute of His attributes, to transfer the matters of His influences and attributes to the matters of the form of the lower realms, that the form should be able to be an analogy hinting to the matters of those influences, and the Master, blessed be He, arranged a complete order that will suffice to make in the forms of the creatures an analogy for all the supernal matters that He wants to show in them, until a proper and complete reason will be found for all the parts of the form of the creatures, that there will not be any matter in them by chance, but everything will be settled on its wheels according to this root - that the supernal and spiritual matters should be hinted at in the forms of the lower creatures themselves. It is from the loftiness of the supernal glory, that the prophet will not comprehend the supernal matters except from the aspect of their relation to the creatures themselves, their being hinted at in them, and as we have explained.

Indeed, there is even more depth in this matter, and it is, that the order and way that the Master, blessed be He, took to transfer with it the matters of influence to the matters of the form of the lower realms, and as we have explained, is what very much acts in the existence of these creatures in all their forms. I will give you an analogy of this, because the Holy One, blessed be He, wanted to transfer the matter of His providence to the matter of the eye, therefore the eye exists in man.

Because He wanted to transfer the attributes of His providence - the attribute of kindness, the attribute of justice and the attribute of mercy - to the matter of the colors white, red and green, therefore these three colors exist in the eye of man. If He would not have wanted to transfer these matters in this way, these limbs and their parts would not be in man, but other limbs and parts, and this is simple. So with all the other constitutions in existences, and their qualities, and their prevailing at times in one way and at times in another way, until they make the changes of states in all created bodies - all this depends on the way how the Master, blessed be He, wanted to transfer the supernal matters to forms and structures in creatures.

It is found, that this matter is a great root for creatures and their occurrences. Therefore, the Master, blessed be He, shows His glory to the prophet in the way of these images, so that he will understand the bestowed attributes, and also their being transferred to the lower forms, so that he will properly comprehend and understand the affectation that is done in the lower realms from the supernal influences in all the orders of the relative value, and all the distinctions that He made in this matter.

It is found, that the prophets will see images of great and small lights, ascending or descending, moving and standing, and various kinds of images like the matters of images of the lower realms, and as we found for them the verses, in their soulful sight, and as we have explained, and from them they will contemplate and stand upon the orders of the supernal influence and governance in all its orders.

Indeed, the indication of the images upon the attributes is according to what is understood from the form itself. For example, the spherical form that surrounds, which has no right or left, no beginning or end, indicates an all-encompassing single outlook that equally surrounds the entire matter that it oversees.

But the straight form that is divided into sides, right, left and middle, and it has a head and feet, indicates a graduated and detailed outlook, that goes from the upper to the lower in gradation in all that are overseen by it, and so in the distinction of the details - these to the right and these to the left, and so all the other forms, all of them.

The explanation of the matter, behold, this lower world is all overseen with a general providence for its existence from the supernal will, and in the aspect of existence there is no difference between species and species, and not between man and man, for the great sphere needs existence like the small gnat. It is found, His providence, equally surrounds all the creatures, all of them, and they are all carried by Him and borne by His power.

But the judicial providence which is for the matter of service, it is a providence that divides into many details, for God, may He be blessed, weighs each thing in the scales of justice to do good or to do bad, each and every thing for a particular reason according to what it is.

When the Master, blessed be He, wants to show His prophets His great power that bears all existence and His providence that encompasses them all equally, with none missing, and none hidden from the eyes of His oversight, He will show him as if a light from Him, may He be blessed, surrounds the entire world, like the firmament that surrounds the earth from all its sides, and so it is said (Ezekiel 1:22), "The likeness of the firmament upon the heads of the living creature," etc.

When He wants to show him His judgment, He will show before his eyes as a king sitting on his throne, righteousness on His right and justice on His left, to establish all His creatures in judgment of His righteousness.

If God, wants to show His prophet the details of the powers that bear the world one above the other, like the matter of what the Sages said (Chagigah 12b), "On what does the earth stand? On the pillars, and the pillars - on the water, etc., and they all depend on the arm of the Holy One, blessed be He" - He will show the prophet many spheres one within the other, each upper one surrounding the lower one beneath it, and the world in the center of them all, and He, may He be blessed, overseeing and bearing them all.

When He wants to show him the chain of all the powers that go in gradation, drawn one from the other, and the lower world drawn from the end of them all, and as we have explained in its place, behold, He will show him levels upon levels one beneath the other, and the world beneath them all.

When He wants to show him the level of elevation of the existences closer to Him, may He be blessed, and those farther from Him - in the order of gradation, and in the attributes themselves that are closer to His perfection, and those that are more distant that relate more to the relative value of the lower realms - He will show him levels upon levels one within the other, like a chamber within a chamber, or like a garment on top of a garment, and the lower world outside of them all, external to them all.

Not only that, but He will show him all these visions at once, if He wants to inform him of all the matters that we mentioned and all their results as one, even though they are contradictory to each other, and like the matter of (Jerusalem Talmud Nedarim 3:2), "The nakedness of your brother's wife" and "her husband's brother shall go in unto her," "Remember" and "Keep," that we mentioned above that are said in one utterance; for what is above nature is not limited by the laws of nature.

Already in a dream, which is also of the type of prophecy, and as the Sages said (Berachot 57b), "A dream is one-sixtieth of prophecy," some of this will occur - that matters will appear that are not according to sight at the time of wakefulness, and the subjects will change for the dreamer in one moment without him discerning the way they changed. A person will see one man in his dream, he will think that he is Reuben, and in one moment he will think that the one he sees is one house or one stone. In short, combinations will be combined that are not at all according to the way of sight. All the more so prophecy which is actually outside of nature, that the Holy One, blessed be He, will use similes through the hand of the prophets as He wants, and as we have already explained above.

Soul: You have settled me very much with these words of yours. Before we complete our discourse, I will ask you a small question that is not so very necessary, but its answer will be pleasant for me.

Intellect: Ask.

Soul: The matter of creation, whether it is possible to understand its way, meaning, how did something come from nothing, or not?

Intellect: How the Holy One, blessed be He, acts, I have already informed you that it is impossible for us to comprehend, meaning, in what way He does His action. We must only inquire into what He acts upon, and in what order He acts. I will answer you regarding what you asked. This matter that He innovated, is an absolute innovation that the Master, blessed be He, innovated with His lofty ability, which it is impossible for us to understand how He innovated it. However, in what order He acted to innovate it - this we can understand, for, in this we only understand the gradation of the action. We will say, that the making of this matter that He made, was certainly prior in His law, that He could make it, and that He was destined to make it, for we cannot think of Him, may He be blessed, any addition or change at all, that any matter should be innovated with Him that He did not have; but it was prior in His will that He would make this matter. However, this is not even called the world being in potential, for there is no relation between His simplicity, and His creatures, and all the appellations that fall upon His creatures do not fall upon His essence, at all. Only when He actually wanted to innovate this matter, then He innovated kinds of influences from Him, may He be blessed, that it was in their law to actually bring forth this matter, and they have a relation to this matter, for they were only innovated in a measure proper to bring forth this matter. Indeed, I have already informed you that these influences are kinds of influences that go in an order of gradation. But only the last and least kind among all the influences will be called a proximate cause to this matter in its constitution as it is. I have already explained this matter to you above very well.

It is found, that since the first influence was innovated, the making of the matter is already in its law, and it is said that this matter is included in it, for it is in the law of its matter, and it was only innovated for it; but it is still a remote cause, for its matter is more honorable and lofty than what is required for the existence of the lowly matter. The second influence will be a more proximate cause to it, and it is more closely included in its law and closer to being found than it is in the first. So in this way it goes and revolves in the laws of all the influences that He innovated for this, and from the last of them it comes out in actuality.

The first influence is nothing, but the existence of this matter influenced from Him, may He be blessed, with greater intensity than is proper to be. The second influence is similarly the existence of this matter influenced with less power than the first. The influences are nothing but the existence of one existent sent forth and influenced from Him, may He be blessed, that until it is sent forth from Him before its result comes out in actuality - it is called an influence from Him. When the matter of the influence comes out in actuality and becomes an existent among the existents - then it is called a result. It is found, the influences and the results are one matter, but the influences are the entirety of His providences, and the results are the existents that are born from the providences. But His providence is like all His other matters, that are not known intrinsically, like His knowledge and His remembrance and His compassion, which are not something outside of Him, and not like our knowledge and our remembrance and our compassion; but they are providences that from the aspect of their action we comprehend them, that they are nothing but the finding of those existents, and the sending forth of the existence of those existents and their essence from Him, may He be blessed. This is sufficient for what you asked.

Soul: I am certainly very, very happy with my portion, that I have received from you great and profound knowledge, and I have remained completely settled in the complete and faithful faith in all the things that every member of the religion of Moshe and Israel must be settled in, and peace be upon Israel. Blessed be the Lord forever, amen and amen.

The Books of the Ramchal

The Ramchal wrote more than eighty books on Kabbalah, ethics, morality, philosophy, and more. Most of his books have been lost and today we are only aware of these books

מסילת ישרים	סוד ה' ליראיו
'דרך ה	תקט"ו תפילות
מאמר העיקרים	תיקונים חדשים
.דרך חכמה	קיצור כוונות
דרך עץ החיים	עיקרי הדינים
דרך תבונות	אגרות רמח"ל
דעת תבונות	ירים משה
ספר הכללים	ספר השירים
קל"ח פתחי חכמה	שרשי המצוות
קנאת ה' צבאות	ספרי דקדוק ומליצה
אדיר במרום	לשון לימודים
משכני עליון	ספר ההגיון
מאמר הגאולה	ספר המליצה
זוהר תנינא	ספר הדקדוק
עשרה אורות	:מחזות קודש
פנות המרכבה	מעשה שמשון
האילן הקדוש	.מגדל עוז או תומת ישרים
מאמר הוויכוח	לישרים תהילה
חוקר ומקובל	בנין עולם
מלחמת משה	פתחי חכמה ודעת
רזין גניזין	

Description of Some Books of the Ramchal

Adir Bamarom

Adir Bamarom by the Ramchal is a commentary on the section Adrah Rabah of the Zohar. which is a seminal text in the study of Kabbalah. The Ramchal aims to clarify and elaborate on the Zohar's teachings. Each section builds upon the previous one, leading the reader to a more profound understanding of kabbalistic thought and concepts.

Derech Eitz Chaim

Derech Eitz Chaim (The Way of the Tree of Life) is a profound guide to Jewish meditation and prayer. It is not divided into chapters in a modern sense but is rather a continuous discourse divided into sections that deal with various aspects of spiritual practice and prayer. The text is aimed at guiding the reader towards achieving a closer communion with the Divine through a deeper understanding and practice of the mitzvot (commandments) and prayer, with a particular focus on the kavanot (mystical intentions).

Hokhmat HaEmet

"Hokhmat HaEmet" (The Wisdom of Truth) is a work about the exploration of Kabbalistic truth and delves into the Ramchal's understanding of divine wisdom as it pertains to the nature of God, creation, and the path to spiritual enlightenment. It also contains a series of discourses on various topics within Jewish mysticism and philosophy.

Messilat Yesharim

Messilat Yesharim - Way of the Justs by Rabbi Moshe Chaim Luzzatto - the Ramchal, Is a classic work of Jewish ethical literature. Written in the 18th century. It is a practical guide to moral and spiritual growth, rooted in the Mussar tradition. It's structured around the steps one must climb to reach spiritual perfection.

Each chapter in "Messilat Yesharim" is designed to be a stepping stone, gradually leading the reader from fundamental concepts to more advanced stages of spiritual growth and moral excellence. This work is characterized by its clarity, practicality, and depth, offering guidance that is as relevant today as it was when it was written.

Klach Pitchei Chochmah

Klach Pitchei Chochmah - 138 Openings of Wisdom is a Kabbalistic text that is complex and dense, containing deep mystical insights into the nature of the divine and the universe. The text is not structured in a typical chapter format, but rather as individual entries or "openings" that explore various aspects of Kabbalistic wisdom. These openings are concise sections, each discussing different elements of the Sefirotic system, the structure of the divine realms, and the interplay between the physical and the spiritual.

Ma'amar HaGeulah

Ma'amar HaGeulah, or "Discourse on the Redemption," is a kabbalistic exposition on the themes of exile and redemption as they pertain to both individual spiritual states and the collective destiny of the Jewish people and the world, particularly those concerning the ultimate redemption or 'Geulah.'

Migdal Oz

Migdal Oz, which translates to "Strong Tower," is another one of the Ramchal's kabbalistic works. The title itself suggests a focus on strength and fortitude in the spiritual realm, likely drawing from Proverbs 18:10, "The name of the Lord is a strong tower; the righteous run into it and are safe." It contains a series of interconnected discussions or essays on various spiritual and mystical themes and also includes intricate discussions of divine emanations and the ways in which they interact with the world and humanity.

Kinat Hashem Tzevaot

Kinat Hashem Tzevaot - "The Zeal of the Lord of Hosts." This work discusses the passionate commitment of God to His purposes and plans, particularly as it relates to the defense of His honor and the fulfillment of His will through the history of Israel and the unfolding of the cosmos. And the divine zeal as it pertains to the rectification and purification of the world, leading to the final redemption.

Sod Hageulah

Sod Hageulah - Secrets of Redemption is in line with Ramchal's kabbalistic philosophy, it likely explores the deeper spiritual dimensions of redemption (Geulah), both personal and collective. It blends profound kabbalistic insights with practical guidance, encouraging readers to live with an awareness of the redemptive process and to participate in it through spiritual growth and ethical conduct. Each section would build upon the last, forming a comprehensive picture of the Ramchal's vision of

Sefer HaKavanot

Sefer HaKavanot, which translates to "The Book of Intentions," is a mystical manual that delves into the kavanot, or specific mystical intentions and meditations, one should have during the performance of Jewish prayers and commandments (mitzvot). The Ramchal, in this text, elaborates on the profound spiritual roots of Jewish practices and how each act can be a conduit for drawing down divine influences and rectifying the various spiritual realms.

Zohar Tinyana

Zohar Tinyana, -The Second Zohar, is an extension of the themes found in the classic Zohar, written in a similar style. The Ramchal uses the form of a mystical commentary to delve deeper into the secrets of the Torah, expanding upon the spiritual and ethical teachings contained within the original Zohar.

Ma'amar HaVikuach

Ma'amar HaVikuach - The Kabbalist and the Philosopher is a philosophical work by the Ramchal. This work is structured as a dialogue between a philosopher and a Kabbalist and is intended to defend the Kabbalistic worldview against philosophical criticisms.

The Ramchal uses this dialogue to reconcile the seemingly divergent paths of rational philosophy and mystical tradition, arguing that Kabbalah provides a deeper understanding of the world that complements rather than contradicts rational thought.

The philosopher in the dialogue represents the rationalist approach, seeking to understand the world through logic and observation. In contrast, the Kabbalist represents the mystical tradition, which includes esoteric knowledge and divine revelation as sources of truth.

Da'at Tevunot

Da'at Tevunot -The Wisdom of Consciouness is one of the major works of the Ramchal. The book is structured as a dialogue between the intellect and the soul, exploring the nature of divine wisdom and justice. It addresses profound questions about God's management of the world, the purpose of creation, the role of mankind, and the process of redemption.

Samples of books of the Ramchal translated by Rav Raphael Afilalo

The Way of the Justs - Mesilat Yesharim
God and his Ways - Derekh Hashem
The Kabbalist and the Philosopher - Meamar Havikuach

The Way of the Justs – Mesilat Yesharim

The Way of the Justs, is a classic work of Jewish ethical literature. Written in the 18th century. It is a practical guide to moral and spiritual growth, rooted in the Mussar tradition. It's structured around the steps one must climb to reach spiritual perfection.
Each chapter is designed to be a stepping stone, gradually leading the reader from fundamental concepts to more advanced stages of spiritual growth and moral excellence. This work is characterized by its clarity, practicality, and depth, offering guidance that is as relevant today as it was when it was written.

The author said: I did not compose this work to teach people what they do not know, but to remind them of what is already known and widely publicized among them. For you will not find in most of my words anything but matters that most people know and do not doubt at all. However, just as these matters are widely known and their truth is clear to all, forgetfulness of them is also very common and prevalent. Therefore, the benefit derived from this book does not come from reading it once, for it is possible that the reader will not find novel ideas in his mind after reading it that were not there before reading it, except a little. Rather, the benefit comes from reviewing it and persevering with it, for these matters that are naturally forgotten by people will be remembered, and one will take to heart one's duty which one overlooks.

If you consider the current state of most of the world, you will see that most people of quick understanding and sharp intellect apply most of their analysis and contemplation to the intricacies of different wisdoms and the depth of theoretical studies, each person according to his intellectual inclination and natural desire. Some exert great effort in studying the creation and nature, while others devote all of their theoretical analysis to astronomy and geometry, and others to crafts. Yet others delve further into the holy, that is, the study of the sacred Torah -- some in the give and take of halachic discussions, some in midrashim, and some in halachic rulings. But few belong to the category that establishes the study and analysis of matters of perfection in divine service, of love, fear, attachment, and all the other aspects of piety (chassidut).

This is not because these matters are not fundamental principles to them, for if you ask them, each one will say that this is the main principle. One cannot imagine a truly wise person for whom all these matters are not clear. Rather, the reason that they do not apply much analysis to it is due to the matters being so well-known and simple to them that they do not see a need to spend much time analyzing them. The study of these matters and the reading of books of this type is left only to those whose intellect is not so sharp and close to being coarse. You will see them diligent in all this and not budging from it, to the point that according to the practice prevalent in the world, when you see a pious individual, you cannot avoid suspecting him of being of coarse intellect.

However, the results of this practice are very detrimental for both the wise and the unwise, for it causes both to lack true piety, making it very rare to find in the world. It is lacking in the wise due to their limited analysis of it, and lacking in the unwise due to their limited grasp of it. As a result, most people imagine that piety depends on reciting many psalms, very long confessions, difficult fasts, and immersions in ice and snow -- all matters with which the intellect is not content and the mind is not at ease.

True piety, which is desirable and pleasant, is far from our conceptual image. It is a simple matter -- that which is not a person's obligation, he does not have in mind. Even though its basic principles are already fixed in the heart of every upright person, if he does not engage in them, he will see their details without recognizing them; he will encounter them without noticing them. See that matters of piety and matters of fear and love and purity of heart are not matters ingrained in a person such that he does not need means to acquire them. People do not find them on their own just as they find all of their natural functions like sleep and wakefulness, hunger and satiety, and all the other functions engraved in our nature. Rather, they certainly require means and strategies to acquire them, and there are also factors that detract from them and distance them from a person. There is no lack of ways to distance their detriments. If so, how can one not need to spend time analyzing this matter in order to know the truth of these matters, to know the way to acquire them and uphold them? From where will this wisdom come into a person's heart if he does not seek it?

Once the need for perfection in divine service and the obligation of its purity and cleanliness has been affirmed by every wise person -- for without these it is certainly not desired at all, but despised and abhorred, as "the L-rd searches all hearts and understands the inclination of all thoughts" (Chronicles 1:29:17) -- how will we respond on the day of rebuke if we were negligent in this analysis and abandoned a matter that is so incumbent upon us, as it is the essence of what the L-rd our G-d asks of us? Is it conceivable that our intellect would toil and labor in analyses that we are not obligated in, in give-and-takes from which we derive no benefit, and in laws that do not apply to us, while we leave the great duty that we owe to our Creator to habit and treat it as rote learned from others? If we did not contemplate and analyze what is true fear and its branches, how will we acquire it and how will we escape from the worldly vanity that causes us to forget it?

Will it not be forgotten and lost even though we know it is our duty? Love, likewise -- if we do not strive to instill it in our hearts with the force of all the means that bring us to it, how will we find it within us? From where will attachment and passion for Him, may He be blessed, and His Torah come into our souls if we do not pay heed to His greatness and His exaltedness, which give birth to this attachment in our hearts? How will our thoughts be purified if we do not strive to cleanse them of the blemishes that the physical nature inflicts upon them, along with all of the character traits that likewise require correction and straightening -- who will straighten them and who will correct them if we do not pay attention to them and do not examine the matter with great precision? Indeed, if we would analyze the matter with true analysis, we would find it in its true form and benefit ourselves, and we would teach it to others and benefit them as well.

This is as Solomon said: "If you seek it like silver and search for it as for treasures, then you will understand the fear of the L-rd" (Proverbs 2:4-5). He does not say, "Then you will understand philosophy, then you will understand astronomy, then you will understand medicine, then you will understand laws, then you will understand halachot," but rather, "Then you will understand the fear of the L-rd." You see that in order to understand fear, you must seek it like silver and search for it like treasures. Indeed, in what we have been taught by our forefathers and in what is well-known to every intelligent person in general terms -- will time be found for all other areas of analysis but not for this analysis? Why should a person not set aside times, at the very least, for this contemplation, if he is compelled to turn to other analyses or pursuits in the rest of his time?

The verse states, "Behold, the fear of the Lord is wisdom" (Job 28:28), and our Sages, may their memory be for a blessing, said (Shabbat 31b): "'Behold' means one, as in Greek they call 'one' hen." We see that fear is wisdom, and it alone is wisdom. Certainly, that which does not involve analysis is not called wisdom. But the truth is that great analysis is needed for all these matters -- to know them truthfully and not by imagination and false reasoning, and all the more so to acquire them and attain them.
One who contemplates them will see that piety does not depend on those matters that the foolish pietists imagine, but on matters of true perfection and great wisdom. This is what Moses our teacher, peace be upon him, teaches us when he says: "And now, Israel, what does the Lord your G-d ask of you, but to fear the Lord your G-d, to walk in all His ways, and to love Him, and to serve the Lord your G-d with all your heart and with all your soul, to keep the commandments of the Lord and His statutes?" (Deuteronomy 10:12). Here he encapsulated all the

elements of the perfection of the service that is desirable to His blessed Name, which are: fear, walking in His ways, love, wholeness of heart, and observing all the commandments.

Fear is the awe of His exaltedness, may He be blessed, such that one fears Him as one would fear a great and awesome king, and is embarrassed before His greatness with regard to every movement that one is about to make, and certainly when speaking before Him in prayer or engaging in His Torah. Walking in His ways includes the entire matter of the rectitude of one's character traits and their correction, and this is what they, may their memory be for a blessing, explained: "Just as He is merciful, so should you be merciful" (Shabbat 133b), and the general principle of all this is that a person should conduct all of his character traits and all types of his actions according to integrity and morality. Our Sages, may their memory be for a blessing, encapsulated it as "All that brings glory to its Maker and glory to him from man" (Avot 2:1), meaning all that leads to the ultimate true good, meaning that its outcome is the reinforcement of the Torah and the betterment of the fellowship of states. Love is that love for Him, may He be blessed, should be instilled in a person's heart to the point that his soul is aroused to do what is pleasing before Him, just as one's heart is aroused to do what is pleasing to his father and mother, and he is distressed if this is lacking on his part or on the part of others, and he is zealous for this and rejoices greatly when he does something of this.

Wholeness of heart means that the service before Him, may He be blessed, should be with purity of intent, meaning for the sole purpose of serving Him and not for any other motive. Included in this is that one should be whole in service and not like one who hobbles between two opinions or like one who performs the commandments by rote, but that one's entire heart should be devoted to this. Observing all the commandments: As its literal meaning, that is, observing all the commandments with all their details and conditions.

Now, all these are general principles that require great explanation. I found that our Sages, may their memory be for a blessing, summarized these parts in a different order, more detailed and arranged according to the necessary progression in acquiring them properly. This is what they said in a baraita, cited in various places in the Talmud, one of them in the chapter "Before Their Festivals." These are their words: "From here Rabbi Pinchas ben Yair said: Torah leads to watchfulness, watchfulness leads to alacrity, alacrity leads to cleanliness, cleanliness leads to separation, separation leads to purity, purity leads to piety, piety leads to humility, humility leads to fear of sin, fear of sin leads to holiness, holiness leads to Divine inspiration, Divine inspiration leads to the resurrection of the dead."

Based on this baraita, I decided to compose this work to teach myself and remind others of the conditions for perfect service, according to their levels. I will explain regarding each one its matters and parts or details, the way to acquire it and what detracts from it, and the way to be vigilant against them. For I will read it, and so will all who find contentment in it, so that we may learn to fear the L-rd our G-d, and our duty before Him will not be forgotten by us. And that which the corporeality of nature strives to remove from our heart, the reading and contemplation will bring to our memory and arouse us to what we are commanded. May the L-rd be our support and guard our feet from being trapped, and may the request of the psalmist, beloved to his G-d, be fulfilled in us: "Teach me Your way, O Lord, that I may walk in Your truth; unite my heart to fear Your Name" (Psalms 86:11). Amen, may this be His will.

Explaining the general obligation of a person in his world

The foundation of piety and the root of complete service is for a person to clarify and verify what his duty is in his world and toward what he should place his outlook and aspiration in all that he toils for all the days of his life. What our Sages of blessed memory have taught us is that man was only created to delight in G-d and to bask in the radiance of His Presence, for this is the true delight and the greatest of all pleasures that can be found. The place of this delight is truly in the World to Come, for it was created with the preparation needed for this.

However, the means to arrive at this desired destination is this world. This is what they, of blessed memory, said (Avot 4:16): "This world is like a vestibule before the World to Come." The means that bring a person to this ultimate purpose are the mitzvot which G-d, blessed be His Name, has commanded us to perform. The place of performing the mitzvot is only in this world. Therefore, man was placed in this world first, so that through these means that are available to him here, he can reach the place that was prepared for him, which is the World to Come, to delight there in the goodness that he acquired through these means. This is what they said, of blessed memory (Eruvin 22a): "Today is for doing them and tomorrow is for receiving reward."

When you contemplate the matter, you will see that true perfection is only attachment to Him, blessed be He, and this is what King David would say (Psalms 73:28): "But as for me, G-d's nearness is my good." And he says (ibid. 27:4): "One thing I ask of the L-rd, that I seek - that I may dwell in the House of the L-rd all the days of my life, etc." For only this is good, and all that people consider good besides this is vain and deceptive foolishness. However, when a person merits this goodness, it is fitting that he first toil and strive with exertion to acquire it. That is, he should strive to attach himself to Him, blessed be He, through the power of deeds that lead to this matter, and these are the mitzvot.

Now, the Holy One, Blessed be He, has placed man in a location where many things distance him from Him, blessed be He, and these are the material desires; if he is drawn after them, behold, he distances himself and moves away from the true good. Thus, he is truly placed amidst the fierce battle, for all matters of the world, whether for good or bad, are tests for man. Poverty on one hand and wealth on the other hand, as Solomon said (Proverbs 30:9): "Lest I become sated and deny and say, 'Who is the L-rd?', and lest I become impoverished and steal, etc." Tranquility on one hand and suffering on the other hand, until the battle is found before him and behind him. If he will be a man of valor and triumph in the war from all sides, he will be the perfect man who will merit to attach himself to his Creator and emerge from this vestibule to enter the palace to bask in the light of life. To the degree that he conquered his evil inclination and desires and distanced himself from what distances him from the good and strove to attach himself to Him, so will he attain Him and rejoice in Him.

If you delve further into the matter, you will see that the world was created for the use of man. However, it stands in great balance. For if man is drawn after the world and distances himself from his Creator, behold, he deteriorates and causes the world to deteriorate with him. But if he rules over himself and attaches himself to his Creator and uses the world only to assist him in the service of his Creator, he elevates himself and the world itself is elevated with him. For it is indeed a great elevation for all creatures to be of service to the perfect man who is sanctified with His sanctity, blessed be He. This is like the matter that our Sages, may their memory be for a blessing, said regarding the light that the Holy One, Blessed be He, stored away for the righteous, and these are their words (Chagiga 12a): "When the Holy One, Blessed be He, saw the light that He stored away for the righteous, He rejoiced, as it is stated (Proverbs 13:9): 'The light of the righteous will rejoice.'"

Regarding the stones that Yaakov took and placed around his head, they said (Chullin 91b): "Rebbi Yitzchak said: This teaches that they all gathered together into one place and each one said, 'Upon me the righteous one will rest his head.'"

Our Sages of blessed memory have indeed alerted us to this fundamental in the Midrash Kohelet (Rabba 7:13), where they said, these are their words: "'See the work of G-d, etc.' (Kohelet 7:13). "When the Holy One, Blessed be He, created Adam the first man, He took him and led him round all the trees of the Garden of Eden and said to him: Behold My works, how beautiful and praiseworthy they are! All that I have created, I created for your sake. Pay attention that you do not corrupt and destroy My world."

In summary, man was not created for his situation in this world, but for his situation in the World to Come. However, his situation in this world is a means for his situation in the World to Come, which is the ultimate purpose. Therefore, you will find that the statements of our Sages, may their memory be for a blessing, are numerous and they all follow one style, likening this world to a place and time of preparation, and the World to Come to the place of rest and eating what is already prepared. This is what they said: "This world is similar to a vestibule" (Avot 4:16), as they said, of blessed memory: "Today is for doing them and tomorrow is for receiving reward" (Eruvin 22a). "One who toiled on Shabbat eve will eat on Shabbat" (Avodah Zara 3a). "This world is similar to dry land and the World to Come to the sea, etc." (Kohelet Rabba 1:15). There are many such statements along this line.

You can truly see that no intelligent person could believe that the purpose of man's creation is for his situation in this world. For what is man's life in this world, and who is truly happy and tranquil in this world? "The days of our years among them are seventy years, and if with might, eighty years; but their pride is toil and pain" (Psalms 90:10) - with many types of pain, illnesses, ailments and troubles, and after all this, death. Not one out of a thousand is found for whom the world grants many pleasures and true tranquility, and even he, if he lives to a hundred years, has already passed and is negated from the world.

Moreover, if the purpose of man's creation were for his situation in this world, there would be no need for instilling in him such an important and lofty soul that would be greater even than the angels themselves, all the more so since it finds no satisfaction in any worldly pleasures. This is what they taught us, of blessed memory, in Midrash Kohelet, these are their words (Kohelet Rabba 6:6): "'And also the soul will not be filled' - To what is the matter comparable? To a villager who married a princess. If he brings her everything in the world, it is worth nothing to her, for she is a princess. So too the soul - if you bring it all the delicacies of the world, they are nothing to it. Why? Because it comes from above."

Similarly, our Rabbis, may their memory be for a blessing, said (Avot 4:22): "Against your will you were created and against your will you were born." For the soul does not at all love this world; on the contrary, it despises it. If so, the Creator, blessed be He, certainly would not create a creation for a purpose that is against its nature and despised by it. Rather, man's creation is for his condition in the World to Come. Therefore, this soul was placed in him, for it is fitting for it to serve, and through it man can receive reward in its place and time, so that nothing despised will befall his soul in this world. On the contrary, it will be loved and cherished by it. This is simple.

Now that we know this, we immediately understand the severity of the mitzvot that are upon us and the preciousness of the service that is in our hands. For behold, these are the means that bring us to true perfection, without which it cannot be attained at all. However, it is known that the goal is not reached except through the power of assembling all the means that were found and that served to reach it. According to the power of the means and their utilization, so will be the goal born of them. Any slight difference found in the means, its outcome will certainly be discerned with clarity when the time of the goal born of the assembly of all of them arrives, as I wrote, and this is clear. From now on, it is certain that the precision with which one must be exacting regarding the mitzvot and service must be with the utmost precision, as weighers of gold and pearls are exacting due to their great value. For their outcome is born in true perfection and eternal preciousness, above which there is no greater preciousness.

We have thus learned that the main existence of man in this world is only to fulfill mitzvot, serve, and withstand trials. The pleasures of the world should not be for him except merely as an aid and assistance, so that he will have contentment and peace of mind in order to turn his heart to this service that is incumbent upon him. Indeed, it is fitting for him that his entire orientation should be only to the blessed Creator, and he should have no other purpose in any act he performs, small or large, except to draw close to Him, blessed be He, and to break down all the barriers that separate him from his Maker. These are all matters of materiality and what depends on them, until he is drawn after Him, blessed be He, literally like iron after a magnet. Whatever he can think of as a means for this closeness, he should pursue it and grasp it and not let go of it.

And whatever he can think of as a hindrance to this, he should flee from it as one flees from fire. As it is said (Psalms 63:9): "My soul cleaves after You; Your right hand upholds me." Since his coming to the world is only for this purpose, namely, to attain this closeness by rescuing his soul from all that prevents it and causes it to lose out, now that we know and have clarified for ourselves the truth of this principle, we must examine its details according to their levels, from the beginning of the matter to its end, as Rabbi Pinchas ben Yair arranged them in his statement that we already cited in our introduction. They are: watchfulness, alacrity, cleanliness, separation, purity, piety, humility, fear of sin, and holiness. Now we will explain them one by one with the help of Heaven.

God and His Ways - Derekh Hashem

Introduction by the Ramchal

The sublime advantage of comprehending reality through grasping the precise configuration and interrelation of its constituent parts, rather than viewing it as an undifferentiated whole, is akin to the difference between observing an orderly garden beautifully arranged into beds, paths and rows, versus seeing a chaotic thicket or tangled forest. For though one may conceptualize many parts whose authentic connections and positioning within the integrated structure remains unknown, this leaves the intellect that yearns for true understanding burdened without satisfaction. Each element pictured in isolation excites curiosity about its completion within the whole, yet its deficient portrayal precludes this, thus troubling the mind and paining it with unquenched longing and unremitting confusion.

In dramatic contrast, one who properly discerns the nature of each part according to its various aspects beholds the subject unveiled before him in its fullness. The intellect then delights, following wherever interest leads within the beauty of its composition, as coherent comprehension is attained. For integral to properly understanding any topic is recognizing its essence and distinguishing parameters.

Thus, one must firstly determine the fundamental categorization and station of each element within the framework of reality. The primordial classifications are: whole or part; generality or particular; cause or effect; conveyer or addon. Correspondingly, initial analysis of any subject must establish whether it is a complete entity or constituent component; a universal principle or specific detail; an originating cause or resultant outcome; an underlying substrate or accrued attribute.

Profoundly, the precise aspects warranting examination stem from its innate properties and role. If part, one must identify the whole it helps comprise. If particular, its belonging generality is sought. Effects are traced to causes, and causes to antecedents. Adjuncts are scrutinized in light of their bearer. Additionally, the adjunct's nature is examined - whether preceding, following or concomitant; whether essential or happenstantial; potential or extant; etc. For absent such methodical distinctions, no well-formed conceptualization is possible.

Most crucially, the absolute or delimited nature of each matter must be determined, with clear recognition of any relevant parameters. For misconstruing an entity by ascribing inappropriate qualities or considering it out of context engenders misconception. Though particulars may be enumerable only to an infinite intellect, one should strive to understand essential general principles. Since generalities intrinsically contain innumerable details, properly grasping a key universal concept enlightens one to the truth of myriads of particulars subsumed within it, suddenly recognizing each one that becomes known through its self-evident belonging to that broader reality. As our sages advise, "One should always have matters of Torah as generalities, not particulars."

Yet general principles must also be properly understood in their full scope and aspects. No detail is truly negligible or unworthy of concern, for nothing exists devoid of consequence at some level. While some specifics may be irrelevant in certain contexts, their impact elsewhere remains significant, given the all-encompassing nature of each general truth that must suffice in every respect. Careful attention and precise tracing of the progression through which each detail flows from prior elements and coalesces into subsequent effects is therefore imperative, that one may gain true wisdom and enlightenment.

Accordingly, dear reader, I have composed this work to elucidate the foundations of faith and service definitively, in a clear systematic manner facilitating authentic comprehension of these pivotal principles in all their aspects, saved from confusion. Herein their roots and branches are bared, interrelations explained, such that they take root and become absorbed within your heart and soul, for the perfection of your mind and being. From this basis, attainment of the knowledge of God throughout

Torah, and comprehension of all its hidden treasures, will readily unfold through divine blessing.

I have diligently endeavored to present the ideas in a compelling progression, and language optimally expressive, to impart an accurate picture of these essential ideas I wish to share. Therefore, gentle friend, I ask that you likewise examine this work carefully, hold fast to its guidance, and do not overlook any detail, that no indispensable matter elude you. But delve thoroughly into its words to grasp each concept in its full depth of meaning, that its truths permeate your consciousness, and you find the tranquil clarity for which your soul surely yearns.

This text's title, Derech Hashem, meaning "God and His Ways or The Way of God," reflects its focus: the path of divine truth revealed by the prophets and in the Torah, through which He shapes reality and guides humankind. Correspondingly, this work unfolds in four sections: first, the foundations of existence; second, God's providence; third, prophecy; and fourth, proper service. May each word awaken within you vision and understanding, that you may walk amidst the wonders of His wisdom and ways.

Therefore my brother, who genuinely seek closeness with Hashem, take this as your guide, that God be with you. For He bestows discerning eyes and attentive ears to glimpse the hidden marvels embedded in Torah's every layer of meaning.

On the Existence of God

Every Jew must believe and know that there exists a first Being, eternal and everlasting, who brought into existence and continues to bring into existence all that exists, and He is God, blessed be He.

It must also be known that the truth of this Being, blessed be He, is completely beyond grasp by anything other than Him. Only this is known about Him: that He is a perfect Being in all manners of perfection, and absolutely no deficiency exists in Him. These matters we know through tradition from the Patriarchs and Prophets. All of Israel attained them at the event of Mount Sinai and stood firmly upon their truth. They taught them to their children throughout the generations, as Moses our teacher commanded by the mouth of the Almighty—"Lest you forget the things your eyes beheld etc. You shall make them known to your children and grandchildren."[1]

However, all these matters are also proven true by intellectual investigation through conclusive proofs. It will be shown to be necessary that they are so, from the existent beings and their conceptions that we see with our eyes, according to the science of nature, geometry, astronomy, and other sciences. From them will be taken true premises which will yield a demonstration of these true matters. However, we will not elaborate on this now, but only present the premises for their truth. Then, we will arrange the matters clearly, according to the tradition in our possession and what is well known throughout our nation.

It must be known that the existence of this Being, blessed be He, is a necessary existence, that it is completely impossible for Him not to exist.

It must also be known that His existence does not depend on anything else whatsoever; rather, His existence is necessary of itself.

Similarly, it must be known that the existence of God is a simple, unique existence without any composition or multiplicity. All perfection exists within Him in a simple manner. Meaning that as it is for the soul, where are found many varied powers, each of which has its own definition. For example, memory is one power, desire is another power, as is imagination, and none of these enters into the definition of the other at all. The faculty of memory is one definition, and desire is another, and desire does not enter into the definition of memory, nor memory into the definition of desire, and so on for all of them.

However, God, blessed be He, does not possess varied powers, even though in truth there are within Him varied matters—for He indeed desires. He is wise, powerful, and perfect with all perfection. However, the truth of His existence is a singular matter that truly includes within its truth and definition—meaning the truth of its matter—that all perfection is necessarily inherent within it and all deficiencies are necessarily absent from it.

It turns out that all perfection exists within Him not as something added onto His essence and the truth of His matter, but rather due to the truth of His matter itself, which includes all perfection within its truth, for it is impossible for that matter to exist without all perfection inherently.
Behold, in truth, this approach is extremely beyond our grasp and conception. We have virtually no way to explain it nor words to expound it. Our conception and imagination encompass only compound matters bounded by the nature created from Him, for that is what our senses sense and bring the conception of to the intellect.

But in creations, the matters are many and separate. However, we have already prefaced that the truth of His existence is beyond grasp. Nothing can be inferred about the Creator from what is observed in creations, for their matters and existence are not at all equivalent such that we could deduce from one about the other. But this too is from the matters known through tradition, as stated, and proven true through investigation of nature itself, in its laws and dynamics.

For it is certainly impossible that a singular Being found, devoid of all nature's laws, boundaries, and limitations; devoid of any absence or deficiency; of any multiplicity or composition; of any relativity or finite measure; and of any of the attributes of creations. He would be the true cause for all existents and all generated within them. For without this, the existence of these beings we observe and their continuity would have been impossible.

It also must be known that this Being, blessed be He, must necessarily be one and no more. Meaning, it is impossible for multiple existents whose existence is necessary of themselves to exist, but only a singular one must exist with this kind of necessary perfect existence. If any other existents are found, they will only exist because He wills them into existence through His will. All existents would depend on Him and not exist of themselves.

It turns out that these foundational cognitions are six, and they are: the truth of His existence, His perfection, the necessity of His existence, His independence, His simplicity, and His unity.

The Purpose of Creation

The purpose of creation is the bestowal of goodness from His own abundance, blessed be He, unto something other than Himself. When you consider this, you realize that He alone, blessed be He, embodies true perfection, completely free from any deficiency. There is no other form of perfection that can compare to His.

Consequently, any form of perfection separate from His is not genuine perfection. It is only termed as perfection in comparison to something that has more flaws. However, absolute perfection is nothing but His own, blessed be He. Thus, His desire to bestow goodness upon another cannot be fulfilled by giving just some goodness; He must give the ultimate good that a creation can receive.

Since He alone is the embodiment of true good, His desire to do good can only be fulfilled by allowing another to partake in that very same inherent good, which is the complete and true good. However, this good is found only in Him. His wisdom, therefore, decreed that the realization of this bestowal should be through providing a space for creations to connect with Him, to the extent of their ability.

This means that although it is impossible for them to attain the same level of perfection as His, by connecting with Him, they can achieve a certain degree of that perfection. They can delight in that true goodness, to the extent that they are capable. Thus, the intention of God in creation is for it to delight in His goodness, to the extent possible.

Nevertheless, His wisdom has determined that for the good to be complete, the recipient of this delight must possess the good themselves. In other words, they must acquire this good on their own, not simply receive it by chance. This resembles, to a certain extent, His own perfection. For He, blessed be He, is inherently perfect, not by chance. Perfection is an intrinsic part of Him, and deficiencies are inherently absent from Him, because of the true nature of His being.

God's wisdom has decreed that for the good to be complete, the one delighting in it must take possession of that good themselves. This means that they must acquire the good through their own efforts, not just stumble upon it. This is a semblance of God's own inherent perfection, not a perfection that just happens to be there. For God is perfect by His very nature, without any deficiencies. His very essence demands perfection and excludes any flaws. However, nothing besides God can possess this inherent nature. To somewhat resemble Him, a being must at least strive for perfection on their own, not have it imposed upon them, and eliminate any potential deficiencies.

Therefore, God has arranged for both perfection and deficiency to be possible outcomes. He created beings with the potential for both, providing them with the means to attain perfection and eradicate deficiencies on their own. In doing so, they resemble their Creator as closely as possible, making them worthy of connecting with Him and delighting in His goodness.

Furthermore, as these created beings strive for perfection and increasingly resemble their Creator, they also draw closer to Him. This process continues until achieving perfection and being in close connection with Him become one and the same. This is because His existence, blessed be He, is the epitome of true perfection. Therefore, any form of inherent perfection belongs solely to Him, like a branch originates from a root. Although the branch may not reach the original perfection of the root, it is nonetheless an extension and result of that initial perfection.

You can see that true perfection belongs only to His existence, and any deficiency is simply the concealment of His goodness and the hiding of His presence. The revelation of His presence and closeness to Him are the root causes of all perfection. Conversely, the hiding of His presence is the root cause of all deficiencies. The degree of His presence determines the level of perfection, and its absence results in deficiency.

Humanity stands balanced, influenced by the revelation or concealment of God's presence. By actively pursuing perfection and acquiring it through their own efforts, humans grab hold of Him, who is the source of all perfection. The more they perfect themselves, the stronger their connection and closeness to Him become. Eventually, the ultimate achievement of perfection and the ultimate closeness to Him become synonymous, resulting in delight in His goodness and true perfection.

For these dynamics of perfection and deficiency to exist, and for humanity to have the capacity for both as well as the ability to acquire one and remove the other – and for the means towards this perfection to be accessible – there must be a myriad of details in creation. These details are interrelated until the ultimate purpose is fully realized.

However, the creation intended for this grand purpose of connection with God is deemed the primary creation. Everything else in existence serves to assist this primary creation in achieving its ultimate purpose.

Specifically, humans represent the true primary creation. All other creations, whether of a higher or lower order, exist solely to aid humanity in fulfilling its complete spiritual purpose in all its varied aspects and requirements. We will delve deeper into this topic later, God willing. For now, understand that wisdom and virtuous character traits are aspects of perfection, meant to refine humanity. Physicality and imagination, on the other hand, are aspects of deficiency, between which humans navigate to achieve their own state of perfection.

The Kabbalist and the Philosopher - Meamar Havikuach

Philosopher: Peace be upon you, my brother! How good is your coming at this time, for I am in great need of you.

Kabbalist: How can a philosopher need a kabbalist? You have already let your thoughts roam all corners of creation and subjugated it under you with your decisive proofs. How can I be of use to you?

Philosopher: Excessive praise is nothing but mockery. Let us come to the matter at hand. I will speak to you with the integrity of my heart, as is the way of our friendship. I have read and heard some matters from your Kabbalah, and they seem quite strange to me, for they contradict my investigations entirely. However, since I saw many pious individuals who followed its ways, I said to myself that I would see what you have to say. Perhaps I will hear from you something that, if not compelling, will at least not be contradictory and foolish according to sound reason, as it currently appears to me, leaving me no choice but to reject it.

Kabbalist: I will do as you say and inform you of the truth as it was transmitted to us by those who know the truth. The entire benefit of this knowledge will be that you receive from me another piece of knowledge: that you know that all a person can grasp through his philosophical inquiry is considered as nothing compared to what he can grasp through the true Kabbalah.

Regarding this, the wise one said: "For the Lord gives wisdom, from His mouth come knowledge and understanding" (Proverbs 2:6). Now open your mouth wide, and I will fill it.

Philosopher: First, I wish to know from you about the sefirot that you mention - what are they? I would like to know this clearly, for I have heard such strange things about them that I had to restrain myself out of respect from crying out in the streets how astonished I was by them. I was nearly forced to say that they are nonsensical matters.

Kabbalist: Tell me what you heard about this.

Philosopher: I heard it said that they are one light that the Emanator, blessed be He, emanated from His primordial light, and that He, blessed be He, garbs Himself within them like a soul within a body.

Kabbalist: What else did you hear about this?

Philosopher: I heard that there is Atzilut, and there is Beriah, Yetzirah, and Asiyah. The difference between them is that Beriah, Yetzirah, and Asiyah are nothing but an illumination from this emanated light that we mentioned, and that it is divided into two parts. The inner part of it, meaning the soul, is called Divinity, while from the soul and below it is no longer called Divinity, but rather the "World of Separation." This applies to all three worlds.

Kabbalist: What do you say about this?

Philosopher: By the life of my soul, I do not even know how to arrange my difficulties due to their great quantity and quality, for this contradicts all reason and the truth of our faith.

Kabbalist: How so?

Four Difficulties Regarding the Sefirot of Atzilut

Philosopher: From now on, you will not escape one of these two options: Either you will say that they are Divinity, or not.

Kabbalist: But you already heard about this, that Atzilut is Divinity.

Philosopher: If it is Divinity, how can you conceive in your mind that Divinity can be derived from Divinity?

You said two things - that this contradicts all reason and our faith.

Philosopher: Indeed, regarding reason, it is as I said. For how can it be conceived that Divinity derives from Divinity? For God, meaning that Unique One who must exist to be the head of all creatures - since they are many, it is impossible for them to be conducted in an equal and fixed order except by a single head over them all. Therefore, we must understand that Unique One as the ultimate unity. How can we conceive of plurality, birth, and derivation of light within Him?

As for faith, tell me now, is this notion so far, God forbid, from the belief of the Christians, may their name be obliterated, who posited the Trinity, saying that He is three and He is one? For the One actually derives progeny from Himself, and yet it is all one. Furthermore, that which is renewed must not have existed prior to its renewal. If you say that the sefirot are new divinity, while the Infinite is ancient divinity, is this not exactly what is said about such things: "They chose new gods" (Judges 5:8)?

Additionally, how greatly do you stumble in faith, for we know that the Holy One, blessed be He, is absolutely simple, unaffected by any bodily contingencies. According to your words, there is no greater contingency than this - that His essence, blessed be He, should transform from non-existence to existence.

Kabbalist: You have already shaken the entire world with your words. Do you have any more such difficulties?
Philosopher: Indeed, I do. For now I spoke in general only about the matter of Atzilut. When we come to Beriah, Yetzirah, and Asiyah - they are exceedingly numerous. In truth, I have such strong questions and difficulties there that no mind of a wise and understanding person can bear them.

Kabbalist: Please state your words, and let me know what you have to say about this.

Difficulties Regarding the Sefirot of Beriah, Yetzirah, Asiyah

Philosopher: When you come to Beriah, Yetzirah, Asiyah, you make a continuum, and still call it Divinity. Afterward, you say that part of it is called Divinity, while part of it is not called by this name. Tell me, by your life, have you ever heard that Divinity could be divided to such an extent that half of it remains Divinity while half of it does not, but rather becomes a subservient slave to the first half? Believe me, faithful friend, these are not words of wisdom. It is impossible to bring such matters to the ears of an intelligent person, only to the simple-minded who believe everything.

However, there are two things I would like to know in any case: First, who involved us in this conflict? Second, what benefit emerges from this knowledge? Is the faith that the entire congregation of Israel believes - that the Creator is One, that He governs His world, that He gave His Torah to us, and that our Messiah will come - not good? What need do we have for all these matters of sefirot and worlds that breed nothing but confusion?

Kabbalist: Please complete your words.

Philosopher: I have one difficulty that encompasses all difficulties - that everything I have read or heard is astonishing from beginning to end. However, I think that if I would find at least one solid foundation upon which all these structures could be built, then perhaps the details would be comprehensible. But without that, why should I toil over the details when the entirety is difficult?

Can a Body Develop from Divinity?

However, I will not refrain from mentioning one strong difficulty I have with their words, which branches into two, but has one root:

I heard that you say that the sefirot developed level by level until this physical world came into being. This is an extremely difficult matter. What sense can there be to these words? How can that which is Divinity develop to the point of becoming one opaque body?

How Can We Understand the Emergence of the Other Side from Holiness?

The second, an even greater and more astounding difficulty, is what they say - that the Other Side emerged from the end of din (justice). Even more astonishing, they say that initially, good and evil were mixed together, and that is why the first worlds were destroyed, until the good was clarified by itself, which are the sefirot of holiness, and the evil by itself, which are the sefirot of the Other Side. To me, this matter seems almost like heresy, God forbid - to say that the Other Side was initially mixed into the sefirot, whether overtly or covertly. Say what you will, but they were one entity. How can one thing be clarified from it, with one part becoming the sefirot, which is Divinity, and the other part becoming the Other Side? I have no heart to accept these matters, and certainly not to utter them, for it seems to me that this leads to the heresy of two authorities, God forbid.

If the Sefirot are Divinity, How Can They Emanate from Divinity?

If you answer that the sefirot are light emanated from the Blessed Infinite One, and that is why such things are possible for them, this was already the first difficulty - how can one say that Divinity emanates from Divinity? If they are emanated from Him, they are outside of Him. Even if you say a hundred times that they are like a flame connected to a coal (Sefer Yetzirah 1:7), these are things said by mouth but are not accepted by the heart. For to say that something that is not essentially divine could still be divine is one of the impossibilities.

How Can We Understand Service Via the Sefirot?
Furthermore, according to your approach, all service is via the sefirot, and I see no permissibility for this. For we cannot escape the following: If they are not Divinity itself, then they must be able to be separate from Him and exist as vessels without light, like a body without a soul. Yet they are still described with the very attributes of Divinity - this is improper. For "the God of gods is the Lord" (Psalms 50:1), meaning the Holy One, blessed be He. According to your ways, it would mean Chesed, Gevurah, Tiferet. According to our faith, it is impossible to use these names for anyone other than the Emanator, blessed be He. Rather, "You shall have no other gods before Me" (Exodus 20:3). If you answer that Divinity cleaves to them to such an extent

that they are called by His name - such a thing should never be uttered, for you would be giving an opening to heretics, God forbid, and even worse.

In summary, these matters are very perplexing. Now, if you have the means to resolve them, if not entirely, then at least some of them, I would rejoice greatly.

Kabbalist: Until now, you have made yourself the witness, the judge, and the litigant. I, too, like you, will place you between Him and me as the adjudicator. Your reason will be the one I anticipate, as will you. But incline your ear and set aside your desire for just a moment, until you receive the true knowledge with a clear mind. Indeed, it requires resolution and conciliation.
Philosopher: Speak, and I shall listen.

Kabbalist: You are mistaken in every respect.

Philosopher: But I have heard many of your Kabbalists speak the very things I said.

Kabbalist: Their words need to be properly understood, not taken superficially.

Philosopher: Now let me hear a clear explanation from you.

This Wisdom Teaches the Unity of God and the Integrity of His Governance with Great Wisdom

Kabbalist: The foundation of this entire wisdom is the unity of the Emanator, blessed be He, that He is one in every way, without any change, plurality, or bodily contingency whatsoever.

Philosopher: The foundation is very good, if it can bear its structure.

Kabbalist: The entire matter of the wisdom of Kabbalah is nothing but an explanation of the attribute of His justice, blessed be He, the order of the laws of governance - how the Holy One, blessed be He, causes and governs all affairs of His world with great wisdom.
Philosopher: If this is what we would find in this wisdom, we would find something great. However, I do not see this wisdom proceeding along this path.

How Can We Understand Development in the Sefirot?

Kabbalist: Did I not tell you that you are mistaken in every respect?

Philosopher: I am stating what I gathered from the matters I read in your texts. I saw that you want to explain the chain of development - how the created being emerges from the Creator, as if the Creator, blessed be He, is the primary substance of the creations, developing from Him Himself. This primary substance gradually develops until it reaches the creations themselves. These are the sefirot and all that you expound upon regarding them. For you say that the Creator, blessed be He, placed His very name and was affected in one way until His own light was found to be affected and progressively developing until the lowest level was found. Now, if this matter could truly be stated, it would be very nice. For this development would certainly be the cause of all existences, and their variations would cause the variations in the world's affairs. Therefore, it would be good to know it, especially since the matter lends itself to attributing to it all the mitzvot and service, for it needs to be ordered according to its good nature. However, as I prefaced, if it could be said - for how can it be said that the light of the Creator, blessed be He, is affected or develops? You yourself have already admitted that contingencies do not apply to the Emanator, blessed be He.

Kabbalist: I acknowledge all this, and on the contrary, this is the foundation of my entire structure - that the Emanator, blessed be He, is not subject to any bodily contingency. But I said that you are mistaken in every respect, and I repeat it. It is impossible to say in any way that His light, blessed be He, is itself affected and develops to the extent that the Creator becomes a creation. Have you never heard that creation is something from nothing? If so, how can development and affectedness be spoken of?

Philosopher: Yes, your words have added water, now see to it that you add flour.

Understanding This Wisdom is Knowing His Governance, Blessed Be He

Kabbalist: But you will see that it is impossible for great sages to err in this, such as those from whom the Kabbalah flows to us. However, I will demonstrate to you that you did not understand anything of what you read. Do you know how to explain these levels mentioned in the sefirot, and all their variations mentioned at all times, what their benefit is in creation? How action and deed will result from them below? But inform me of the details, not generalities. If you know this, you can say that you understood what you read. If not, you will certainly say that you read what you did not understand.

Philosopher: Yes, in general I tell you that they are all matters needed to bring about the development of the world, and that through their differences in their states, they differentiate the affairs of the world. But in particular, I do not know what they are - not the qav (line) or the reshimu (impression), not Adam Kadmon, nor his worlds, the tikunim (rectifications) of the partzufim (visages) and their garments and intervals - all these are numerous. These are things I have read but do not know their nature. I only see great difficulties in them.

Kabbalist: If so, you do not know. I will start you on one path so you may see what you had not considered in these matters.
Philosopher: Speak.

Infinite and Sefirot - What He Can Will and What He Willed

Kabbalist: The Emanator, blessed be He, is certainly the Master of will, according to what He willed and wills. Now we can speak of Him in two aspects: in terms of His essence and in terms of His will. Do you admit this or not?

Philosopher: Certainly, we can speak about any subject in terms of each aspect of it independently. For example, when speaking about a person's affairs, the person is called the subject of the discussions, meaning the qualities being discussed about him are called the aspect or aspects of him. We can discuss an aspect of the person - that he is learned, charitable, or wise. Each of these is an independent aspect that we can discuss regarding each subject on its own.

Kabbalist: Regarding the essence of the Emanator, blessed be He, we are forbidden to speak of it, and we do not even need to delve into it at all. For it suffices us to know of His existence. When we know that He is the ultimate perfection, that He is omnipotent - we know what we need to know in this matter. Beyond this, we are already forbidden to even speak. Therefore, we will no longer speak of His essence, only of His will, for this is closer to us and is permissible, as we are not touching upon His essence at all.

Philosopher: It is good to speak of His will. But what can you say? His will has no end, His thought has no limit. What can you investigate regarding that which has no bounds or finitude?

Kabbalist: This is precisely what I wanted to elicit from you, that you admit that there is no end to His will and thought. From now on, you will not be able to flee from me concerning what I wish to impart to you. Please tell me, you certainly believe in reward and punishment, for it is one of the fundamentals of faith. But tell me: There are deeds in the world for which the Holy One, blessed be He, desires to benefit their doers, and there are those for which He desires to punish.

There is a time when He elevates and a time when He lowers; a time when He impoverishes and a time when He enriches. If so, in His will there is certainly a will of beneficence, a will of harm, a will of lowering, and a will of elevating. All this is certainly in order, for there is an order to the governance. If so, we can certainly discuss all of this, as we are not touching upon His essence, blessed be He, at all. In summary, these are the attributes of His will that we can certainly investigate and know.